The McGill Movement

CRITICAL VIEWS ON CANADIAN WRITERS

CRITICAL VIEWS ON CANADIAN WRITERS

The McGill
Movement: A. J. M. SMITH
F. R. SCOTT AND LEO KENNEDY

Edited and with an Introduction by
PETER STEVENS

THE RYERSON PRESS
TORONTO WINNIPEG VANCOUVER

SBN 7700 0294 3

PRINTED AND BOUND IN CANADA
BY THE RYERSON PRESS

CONTENTS

Introduction vi

INTRODUCTION

Most individual authors object strenuously when they are
named as members of a group. They like to be considered
on their own terms rather than on the terms of a loosely
defined group. And there is some justification for a writer's
hostility to being "placed" in this way, for most groupings
do not have a set program but simply an agreement about
general aims. The McGill Movement is perhaps a little
more cohesive in its agreement about general aims: Smith
and Scott were the moving spirits and main contributors
of poetry to the *McGill Fortnightly Review* and Kennedy
joined them a little later. They continued as a group by
contributing to the short-lived *Canadian Mercury* whose
subscribers were passed on to *Canadian Forum* together
with most of the contributors. It could be argued that per-
haps A. M. Klein should be included in this grouping but,
as his poetry and a novel make use of specifically Jewish
themes, I think it is more convenient to treat him as a
separate entity.

Not that Smith, Scott and Kennedy do not have distinct
poetic personalities as well, but in general they do seem to
have had from those early days a similarity in their general
aims. Their poetry was in the nature of a critical rejection
of overblown romanticism in Canadian verse taken over
from late-Victorian and Edwardian sources. Poets through-
out the 1920s with one or two exceptions were writing a
kind of Canadian equivalent, I suppose, of the English
Georgian Movement. The McGill poets drew much of their
material and methods from imagism and its development,

particularly in the work of Eliot. This interest led them to the French symbolists, Metaphysicals and Yeats, and to all the trappings derived from Eliot's poetry and criticism; in Kennedy's case, of course, to a complete immersion in the mythology expounded in *The Golden Bough*.

I have called the initial impulse towards these new ideas about poetry a "critical rejection" and have also suggested that Eliot's criticism played some part in this McGill poetry. In fact, one of the key concepts in the McGill Movement is one of criticism. The editorial in the first issue of the *McGill Fortnightly Review*[1] claimed that the journal's existence was really fostered by "a new and more lively spirit of criticism." The critical spirit manifested itself in literary articles and reviews defending such figures as O'Neill, Eliot and Mencken, and the basis of the theory behind much of the poetry was outlined to a large extent in essays by Smith on "Symbolism and Poetry" (an account of the use of symbols in Herbert, Dickinson, Verlaine and Yeats) , "Contemporary Poetry"[2] and "Hamlet in Modern Dress" (a commentary on Eliot's "The Waste Land") . There is an admonitory tone in much of Smith's prose at this time, culminating in his essay "Wanted—Canadian Criticism"[3] which appeared in the *Canadian Forum* of April, 1928. So schoolmasterish seemed this writing to F. R. Scott that it led him to rebuke Smith in a letter published two months later. This kind of finger-pointing criticism continued throughout Smith's career, resulting eventually in the disagreement between him and John Sutherland who took exception to Smith's division of Canadian poetry into the two strains of "native" and "cosmopolitan" in *The Book of Canadian Poetry* (1943) . Sutherland attacked this view in editorials in *First Statement* and at length in his Introduction to his anthology

---

[1] November 21, 1925.
[2] Reprinted in Louis Dudek and Michael Gnarowski, eds., *The Making of Modern Poetry in Canada* (Toronto: Ryerson, 1967), 27-30.
[3] Reprinted in *The Making of Modern Poetry in Canada*, pp. 31-33.

of the new poetry in Canada 1940-1946, *Other Canadians* (1947) . Smith's views have moderated somewhat in recent years but there are signs of this concept throughout his work, a concept that Padraig O Broin analyzes in his "After Strange Gods," included in this collection.

This critical response also forms part of Smith's earlier poetry. In some of the slight imagist poems he wrote, Smith seemed unable to resist imposing an almost didactic comment (see particularly the poem "Something Apart" in the December 1, 1926 issue of the *McGill Fortnightly Review*) , although most of these poems remain uncollected, Smith obviously finding them of slender value. And of course there is some criticism of society in very general terms in such early uncollected poems as "Cavalcade" and "Testament," and also in "The Face" and "Son-And-Heir." This kind of criticism is more apparent in F. R. Scott's work in his satiric poetry and in some of the hortatory sections of his poetry—one thinks of such a poem as "Overture." Kennedy's criticism is contained in an essay in *Canadian Mercury* about "The Future of Canadian Literature,"[1] condemning the continuance of Victorianism in much Canadian writing. The poems contained in his volume *The Shrouding* (1933) were attempts to bring something new into Canadian poetry; he was to say later that it was an attempt to set "the fertility myth and rites that you find in Frazer's *Golden Bough* in a Canadian dress." This remark occurs in "Direction For Canadian Poets" (see p. 11ff. in this collection), an essay that shows the surprising turn Kennedy's ideas about poetry took in the mid-1930s. Besides making a case for a much more socially conscious poetry in Canada, he rejected all this *Shrouding* poetry as lacking "contact with the larger reality." From then on Kennedy's verse became specifically political in content and in the most part was written in free verse.

---

[1]Reprinted in *The Making of Modern Poetry in Canada*, 34-37.

Both Smith and Scott indulged in critical attacks on literary figures and groups, Scott in book reviews of such poets as Bliss Carman[1] and Stephen Vincent Benét as well as in some of his verse satires and pastiches. Smith used parody (a form of criticism) in many of his poems, taking on the masks of such poets as Yeats, Edith Sitwell and Vaughan. These poems are not always to be regarded simply as light verse—one remembers that Smith has edited an anthology of "serious light verse."

Smith, in fact, has always been a chameleon-like poet, adopting poses and poetical stances to indulge in exercises in poetry. Some of his religious poetry comes into this category, a fact that is not dwelt on sufficiently by W. E. Collin in his chapter on Smith in *The White Savannahs*, a pioneering and valuable book of criticism, making a critical estimate of the major figures then appearing in Canadian poetry. Some of the essays in the book were based on articles he wrote for *Canadian Forum*, including the chapter on Leo Kennedy which later became "This Man of April" in *The White Savannahs*. I decided to include the *Canadian Forum* article rather than "This Man of April" as this earlier essay represents a summation of Collin's ideas about Kennedy's poetry then appearing in the journals of that time; most of them were to appear (without any fundamentally different poems being added) in *The Shrouding*. This essay is also probably less accessible than the chapter in *The White Savannahs*. I have also included a later essay by Collin on Smith, rather than the chapter on Smith in his book—it is perhaps a more considered piece of writing in view of the fact that Smith had by then published his collection *News of the Phoenix* (1943) in which he had already begun his own selection of the poems he wished to preserve.

Poses and masks (and I don't intend these terms to be taken in any derogatory way) were indeed a part of the

[1]*Canadian Mercury*, June 1929, 140 and March 1929, 89-90.

make-up of all these poets: Smith and Scott in their poems in the *McGill Fortnightly Review* used a variety of noms de plume and adopted on occasions different poetic voices; Kennedy's political poems nearly always appeared under the pseudonyms of Arthur Beaton and Leonard Bullen. In fact, one suspects that all three may have parodied one another or even decided to attempt to write poems on a set theme, an impression gained when one sets together almost any of Kennedy's *Shrouding* poems with such poems as Smith's "Undertaker's Anthology" and Scott's "Calvary."

I don't think there has been any really adequate criticism of Canadian poetry of the 1930s because it has always been measured against the English poetry of that period and been found wanting. It seems to me that this is a misguided critical stance, for in no sense did the poets in Canada in the 1930s feel as closely knit a movement as the Spender-Auden-Day Lewis-MacNeice group. Nor did our poets really congregate around specific magazines (perhaps *New Frontier* was the one attempt in Canada to organize a coherent centre of writing) and there was no outlet for poets in Canada equivalent to the variety of poetry magazines in England. Of course the English influence was felt, particularly in Smith's poems of this period and in some by Dorothy Livesay, but in general there is a different tone and texture to Canadian political poetry in the 1930s, ranging from the matter-of-fact series of "Social Notes" by Scott to the rhetorical flights in free verse of Leo Kennedy.

Since that time Kennedy has dropped out of the Canadian poetry scene, Smith has gone on refining and reshaping his poems and assessing and defining Canadian poetry indefatigably in a series of remarkable anthologies, and Scott has been involved in new movements in Canadian life in the fields of both politics and poetry. Indeed, he is a member of the Royal Commission on Bilingualism and Biculturalism; he has always shown a keen awareness of the problems of his native Quebec and has written some fine translations of French-Canadian poems. Smith has demonstrated his fascination with French verse by his inclusion of French-Canadian writing in *The Oxford Book of Canadian Verse* and by his translations of Mallarmé and Gautier. This interest led me to include part of a letter from Scott to Anne Hébert about the problems of translation, as well as an essay by W. E. Collin in French on the poetry of Smith.

Although Smith and Scott are now firmly established as important poets in Canadian poetry of the twentieth century, they have not always been so heralded. Even such a generally perceptive critic as E. K. Brown had some harsh things to say about *New Provinces* when it first appeared, although he changed his opinion later in the 1940s, as he seems to have recognized the far-reaching effects their verse was having on Canadian poetry.

Kennedy has been paid little critical attention. W. E. Collin was a staunch admirer of his work but, apart from this interest, there have been only short notices and reviews and, to my knowledge, no published criticism of his political poetry. He has indeed faded from view over the last twenty-five years or so.

Even as Smith and Scott were gaining some recognition, their poetry was still used in the 1940s as a kind of springboard for polemical criticism, particularly in the dichotomy of *First Statement* and *Preview* and in the controversy centering on the terms "native" and "cosmopolitan." Dorothy Livesay summarized Smith's poetry as having "lack of range, absence of rhetoric, an attitude of withdrawal," and finally asserted that "in the present mood of the world, such poetry will not give sustenance or direction." The *Canadian Poetry Magazine* dismissed Scott's *Overture* by saying that at least half of it was "ungraced by either imagination or wit"; one poem was singled out as "a naked fomenting of class hatred".

And yet in the 1950s critics like Desmond Pacey in

Creative Writing in Canada began to place these poets in the context of the development of modern poetry in Canada and to devote a good deal of time to critical appraisal of their work. Pacey developed the necessarily limited work on Canadian poetry that appeared in *Creative Writing in Canada* in a later book, *Ten Canadian Poets*. This volume places both Smith and Scott in the company of earlier and later Canadian poets, showing their relation to the development of poetry in this country. Pacey's study of these poets is still of great value to the student of Canadian poetry now, eleven years after its first publication. Indeed, it has recently been reprinted in a paperback edition (1966). In this work Desmond Pacey concentrates on biographical information, together with some general groupings of individual poems, in a discussion of the principal themes and techniques used by Smith and Scott. It also contains a good selective bibliography. In view of the fact that the book is now readily accessible, I have not reprinted his chapters on these two poets in this collection, although I have included all relevant information about these chapters in the bibliography.

Occasionally Smith and Scott were seen in a broader context, as in Louis Dudek's discussion of Scott included here. In the 1960s the literary journal *Canadian Literature* has devoted two special issues to the work of Smith and Scott.

Even in the most adverse criticism (as in Lionel Kearns' dismissal of Smith in his review of Smith's *Poems, New and Collected* as being of no relevance in the world of poetry in the middle 1960s), there is still an acknowledgment of the deliberate craft and sharp intelligence of both Scott and Smith. For the last forty years or so, then, it is obvious that they have been in the minds of both practitioners and critics of Canadian poetry. Earle Birney has summarized the effect of the McGill Movement on Canadian poetry in a succinct way. No one who has studied

Canadian poetry can quarrel with his statement about the *McGill Fortnightly Review:*

Short-lived, it yet existed long enough to launch some of the best poets to write in Canada in this century, and eventually to influence, by stimulus or reaction, most of what poetry has succeeded it in the country.

Peter Stevens

Saskatoon, Saskatchewan
1969

THE MONTREAL GROUP

E. K. BROWN

In Montreal, shortly after the end of the First World War, a vigorous group of undergraduates conducted an excellent magazine, *The McGill Fortnightly*. In it appeared the poems of A. J. M. Smith, Leo Kennedy, Abraham Klein, and Frank Scott, all experimenters, eager to naturalize in Canada the kind of poetry then being written by Eliot and Pound, all zealots for the metaphysical verse of the seventeenth century and for Emily Dickinson. From their fellowship was to come long afterward the anthology *New Provinces: Poems by Several Authors* (1936), in which two Toronto poets, Mr. Pratt and Robert Finch also appeared. Two of the Montreal group have brought out volumes of their verse, Leo Kennedy *The Shrouding* (1933), and Abraham Klein *Hath Not a Jew* (1940)....

Frank Scott, now professor of Constitutional Law in McGill University and one of the leading humanitarian idealists in Canada, began with delicate lyrics of exquisite imagery and muted sound; he has since filled his verse with a warm and angry concern for social injustice and social reform. Sometimes, wishing to appeal to a large and relatively uneducated audience, he has striven for a simplicity which is almost unpatterned; again he has contrived to find for his social ideas forms at once simple and beautifully designed. Leo Kennedy, whose Catholic training combined incongruously but effectively in his earlier

From "The Development of Poetry in Canada" by E. K. Brown. From *Poetry*, LVIII (April 1941), 43-5. Copyright 1941 by The Modern Poetry Association. Reprinted by permission of the estate of E. K. Brown and the Editor of *Poetry*.

poems with his fascination by *The Golden Bough* and the
books of Jessie Weston, has come in his maturity to a
more original manner, exhibiting a power of lusty song in
which imagery and diction recalling the metaphysical
poets is at the service of strong feeling and eager thought.

Recognized from the outset as the central figure in the
group, A. J. M. Smith proceeded from McGill to Edin-
burgh where he undertook graduate studies in the poetry
of the seventeenth century with the counsel of Sir Herbert
Grierson. A professor of English at Michigan State College,
he has shown the most acute critical sense of all Canadian
poets; and in an article contributed to what is perhaps the
main critical journal of Canada, *The University of To-
ronto Quarterly*, he sets forth the critical tenets of the
younger poets with vigorous simplicity:

Set higher standards for yourself than the organized medi-
ocrity of the authors' associations dares to impose. Be
traditional, catholic and alive. Study the great masters of
clarity and intensity. . . . Study the poets of today whose
language is living, and whose line is sure. . . . Read the
French and German poets whose sensibility is most in-
tensely that of the modern world. . . . Read, if you can, the
Roman satirists. . . .

And remember lastly that poetry does not permit the
rejection of every aspect of the personality except intui-
tion and sensibility. It must be written by the whole man.
It is an intelligent activity, and it ought to compel the
respect of the generality of intelligent men. If it is a good,
it is a good in itself.

This pronouncement, with which his article concludes,
would, I believe, satisfy almost all the younger poets, those
in the Montreal group and most of the others yet to be
considered.

The principles he sets forth are embodied in Mr.
Smith's own verse. Much of this is acutely religious, some-
times in the metaphysical manner, sometimes more in the
tone of Hopkins. Some of it is coldly satirical, some politi-

cally intense, more politically disillusioned. Little of it has to do with nature, although Mr. Smith has an eye not far inferior to Lampman's for natural detail. Whatever the theme, the execution is beautifully deliberate, and the feeling or thought fully mature and intense. . . .

THE THIRTIES GROUP

R. E. RASHLEY

The *McGill Fortnightly Review* was introducing the work of A. M. Klein, F. R. Scott, A. J. M. Smith, and Leo Kennedy in 1926 and 1927. By 1936, the new movement had become sufficiently self-conscious and successful to publish the anthology, *New Provinces,* adding Robert Finch and E. J. Pratt to the four Montreal poets. . . .

The preface to *New Provinces* was an interesting comment on the conditions out of which the new movement arose. It pointed to the achievement of the "new poetry" as a development of new techniques and a widening of poetic interest, clearly indicating the decline of a tradition and the search for new leads. The modern poets had found an inadequacy in the current material of poetry and sought a content more satisfying to the changing concept of life. The search was not successful and the movement found itself defeated by the aimlessness of its times. The old, nature-as-spirit guide to interpreting experience had lost its validity and left a dissatisfaction and disillusionment with the traditional art. The disillusion was general, in all

"The Thirties Group" by R. E. Rashley. From *Poetry in Canada: The First Three Steps* by R. E. Rashley. Copyright 1958 by R. E. Rashley. Reprinted here by permission of the author and The Ryerson Press. The pages reprinted here are only part of Chapter 8, "The Thirties Group, The Third Step" and part of Chapter 9, "The Significance of the Thirties Poetry."

aspects of life, and all influences from abroad seemed to strengthen it. There was a general casting about for significance, for absolutes around which experience might be organized.

The result was the re-entry into Canadian poetry of the manner and content of contemporary English and American poetry, the discarding of the sixties impressionism and either the refusal of nature as content or a new use of nature. The emphasis was upon mind rather than emotion and the style became metaphysical and psychological, witty, terse, contrived, sometimes contorted, deliberately avoiding the easy melody of the preceding poets and developing an appropriate new vocabulary to avoid the music of the past. The depression focussed attention on man, his nature, and the fruitful organization of life with an immediacy and urgency that absorbed all other interests, gave life again the appearance of common direction and turned this new technique almost immediately and uniformly toward the handling of social content. . . .

Kennedy turned to nature as symbolic of fertility and proceeded from a concept of love as an especial richness of life to love as a guide to the organization of life, in a poetry which seems exotic and literary in its quality, not sustained nor sustaining. . . .

F. R. Scott passes from a concept of love as a meaning below which life fell to a vigorous pronouncement of love as the inspiration of social consciousness, and from a small, sharply delineated poetry to a loose, less-developed structure devoted to persuasion, surface clarity and demonstration which suffers from a conviction that art is less important than the content of art. This poetry is notable for its wit in satire, its close relation to the life around it, and the recurrence of surprisingly different poetic types in the two published collections. Scott sees life as a Dali-esque montage of good and bad in which we are individually responsible for the achievement of social justice. A. J. M. Smith explained man's dilemma in terms of religion and emphasized an understanding of man's nature as "a divided and sinful creature." His reading of life as strung tautly between sense and spirit like the archer's bow requires a somewhat hard and restrained manner which is, however, as in "Tree," capable of tenderness. The critical subjects are the implications of man's failures because he is a man rather than social or commercial organization, again with love as a guide. . . .

The new poetry, dedicated to man and his affairs, tried for cut or bite, for arresting quality, for expression of the mind, for something of the quality of speech. Wit, irony, ingenuity, satire, these are qualities of the intelligence. . . . Finch, Scott, Klein, Smith, and Kennedy are all metaphysicals, in a sense. They are not highly complex and complicated individuals but their style assumes to be complex and complicated in its use of imagery. It is the mind which composes, and the boast of this poetry is that it satisfied the intelligence. Practically all of the poets of this group were partly satirical and destructive, some almost entirely, and the satire was often good. This was a new capacity for Canadian poetry. . . .

In the effort to give the thirties movement roots, Smith imposed the concept of a double stream of tradition on Canadian poetry, the one tradition created by those who had been concerned with national content and the other by those who had sought a content of universal ideas. What Smith was chiefly concerned with was the destruction of the "national" concept of Canadian poetry and the demonstration that the poets of the thirties were part of a total English-language culture and engaged in creative effort that had the sanction of Canadian tradition. While this critical revaluation is made very much from the centre of the thirties' theory of poetry and has the resulting aberrations of vision it is nevertheless a very usable survey of Canadian verse. It succeeded, in conjunction with E. K. Brown's *On Canadian Poetry*, in establishing the thirties movement, its theory and practice of poetry and its critical tenets, at a relatively early stage in the development of the movement. . . .

THE MONTREAL POETS

LOUIS DUDEK

To the envy of less happy cities—Toronto, Halifax, Victoria—one of the particularities in the development of English poetry in Canada over the past thirty years has been the dominant role of Montreal as a center of activity and a source of new poetry. Of the poets who have taken up residence in Montreal for an important phase of their career, or who have been bred here from the start, the list includes the principal names in the modernist school. The main literary magazines, also, containing the program of modern poetry in Canada, have come from Montreal. Work along the same lines elsewhere has often taken its rise from the example of Montreal. Not that Montreal invariably turns out the best poetry; far from it. E. J. Pratt (Newfoundland and Toronto) is still the most accomplished poet we have, with the most solid body of work behind him; Earle Birney is a dominant figure in B.C.; James Reaney, Anne Wilkinson, and Jay Macpherson have appeared at other outposts, although Miss Macpherson has left a touch of Montreal's magic wand (by work and study in McGill's Redpath Library) : these hold their own beside the best poets from Montreal. But Montreal poets include the key figures in the development of modern poetry as a definite tradition in Canada, opposed to the sentimental-genteel poetry of the old culture. The reasons for Montreal's special role in poetry has often been a matter for speculation—not that the problem is a very momentous one, it is no doubt only a form of self-congratulation—yet a few further self-indulgent reflections on the subject may be entertaining, or even useful.

"The Montreal Poets" by Louis Dudek. From *Culture*, XVIII (1957), 149-154. Copyright by *Culture*. Reprinted by permission of the author and *Culture*.

Although it is the largest city in Canada, Montreal is not a central metropolis in relation to this country in the way that Paris or London are cultural capitals of their countries. The thin ribbon of Canadian life stretching along the border of the U.S. from Pacific to Atlantic could hardly have a physical center of any kind. The bow of the ribbon is really in southern Ontario, and Toronto is the economic knot that keeps it neatly tied. Montreal, moreover, is predominantly French in population, so that poetry in English would hardly be expected to find its natural home here. The English-reading audience for poetry in this city is veritably non-existent, and the newspapers habitually ignore poetry in their review pages. How does it happen, then, that Montreal has sprung forth a whole branch of twentieth-century poetry in English within the last three decades?

The scope of this achievement is worth noting. Contemporary poetry in Canada takes its origin from the work of three poets beginning in the late 1920s, A. J. M. Smith, F. R. Scott, and A. M. Klein, all three of them graduates of McGill University. Their work developed through the thirties, appearing in the *McGill Fortnightly* and in the collection *New Provinces* (1936), the latter edited by F. R. Scott in Montreal; the movement then went through a sudden expansion in the early 1940s, stimulated by the Montreal magazines *Preview, First Statement, Northern Review*, bringing out the poets P. K. Page, Patrick Anderson, Irving Layton, and a half-dozen others. It was in *First Statement* that I first appeared, and I was for a time one of the editors of the magazine. The publication of a score of important books, anthologies, and studies of Canadian poetry mark this major phase of the movement. Since then, Montreal poetry has brought into prominence other poets, notably Phyllis Webb, Eli Mandel, and at present Leonard Cohen and Daryl Hine. Other names decorate, or have decorated, the way of advance, among them Leo

Kennedy, Bruce Ruddick, Patrick Waddington and Miriam Waddington.

At its best—and a good anthology of Modern Canadian Poetry has not yet been compiled—this poetry ranks on a par with work from England and the U.S. since 1930. (We have nothing near or equal to Auden, true; as to Dylan Thomas, I think he is a much smaller figure than most people have imagined.) The comparison for Canadian poets would be with Spender, MacNeice, Barker, Karl Shapiro, Jarrell, etc., excellent poets in their kind, but not over-shadowing presences. We have individual poems to match the best of theirs: an achievement that most Canadian readers and reviewers seem to know nothing about. This modern poetry in Canada amounts to a complete body of literature; it is the third sizeable harvest of poetry we have produced, the first being that of Carman, Roberts, D. C. Scott, and Lampman, the second that of Service, Drummond, and E. J. Pratt.

One way to guess at the possible reasons why Montreal has played so important a part in this development is to look at the nature of the poetry coming from this city. . . . I do not say that Montreal poets have on the whole done a very thorough job of depicting or projecting their city in poetry, nor that this is the main source of their strength; but a certain advantage has come to Montreal poetry from the physical tumult and discords of this great city, and from the impulse of the poets, sometimes as a modernist program, to get it down on the page. . . .

The mixture of races—French Canadian, Jewish, English, Irish, Scotch, with several communities of other nationalities (10 per cent) —has given Montreal poets a social kaleidoscope of diverse interest which they have occasionally exploited. Klein has made a definite program of it, one would think, in *The Rocking Chair*. Elsewhere it lies scattered in a fragmentary form, or as background, in the books of the poets, a vein never sufficiently worked, but offering a perpetual stimulus as variety of experience to anyone living in Montreal.

With the mixture or superposition of races, the exact degree of development, or rather lack of development, in our cultural relations is just enough to make the poets feel the lack bitterly, and want to supply it, or curse their fate for failure to do so. The intellectual stagnation of Canada as a whole has a special tang for the poets in Montreal, because here the possibilities of a rich cultural growth are frustrated by ignorance, laziness, hollow tradition, and immovable conservatism. . . .

Montreal poetry, in fact, has been characteristically satirical. F. R. Scott is of course the chief wit; but not one of the fifteen or so poets of the last three decades has omitted to make his sardonic social comment. Where the rest of the country is either settled into traditional conformity or wastes in a bookless and mindless semiliteracy, Montreal has produced poets who are social critics and poets of protest (Layton, Anderson, Scott, etc.), because our "cosmopolitan culture" is forever in that state of simmering, never of boil, that is just enough to exasperate an active mind.

In his recent book, *The Eye of the Needle*, F. R. Scott has this bilingual barb of wit:

It was a big parade.
The floats were big.
Such lovely old costumes!
There were big bands.
And delegates in top hats
From St. Hyppolyte de Kilkenny
And Ste. Suzanne de Boundary Line.
In front were all the leaders
Leading,
While behind came all the followers
Following,
And the cheery crowds gave cheers
Content with all their yesteryears.

Having said this much, one remembers that poetry in Canada, in the period since 1925 when Montreal became the stage for most of the new work, has undergone a transition from a late-romantic poetry, rooted in a Loyalist genteel culture and in moral-religious optimism and puritanism, to the cosmopolitan and exploratory poetry of American modernism. In this transition, Toronto could hardly serve. Fredericton, Kingston, Ottawa might catch on later, but could not possibly begin the break-up. Montreal, having the advantages of a loose miscellaneous society, has therefore provided the setting for a radical change in taste which has since passed or is passing to the rest of the country.

But all these reasons for our poetic vitality are obvious enough; they are the first that would come to mind in any discussion—and they are still not the right ones. One might say that it is all simply a matter of chance, the lucky occurrence at one time (1927) in one place (McGill) of three poets: A. M. Klein, A. J. M. Smith, and F. R. Scott. Before these poets set to work, a Torontonian, W. W. E. Ross, had already written poems for Marianne Moore's *Dial*, clean speedy modern poems that had learned a diction and form from Miss Moore, from William Carlos Williams, and from Cummings. Ross had anticipated our Montrealers; but he had no assistants.

What makes a literature is the contact between one poet and another, between one generation and another. Poets breed by scission. Even when they disagree, they learn, and stimulate one another. Nothing stimulates a beginning poet more than the irritating activity of another poet in his vicinity. And once this local decoction has been started, it perpetuates itself—it can hardly be stopped.

What happened in Montreal is that the first three modernists passed on their impulse—to Leo Kennedy, to Bruce Ruddick, to P. K. Page; they were joined by Patrick Anderson from Oxford, England, and that period is a whole story in itself; this joint activity roused John

Sutherland into competitive emulation (as the literary war between *First Statement* and *Preview* clearly showed) ; the magazines brought out many poets, among them myself, Layton, and the Waddingtons (who came to Montreal from Toronto, during the literary story) ; and since then other poets, Phyllis Webb, Leonard Cohen, Eli Mandel, Gael Turnbull, Daryl Hine, Al Purdy, have been drawn into the Montreal cycle. All this may seem very simple, but it is, in brief, the outline of a complete literary evolution, with about fifty volumes of poetry to make it monumental. It is still open territory for a good critic.

The theory of literature here would be that there is no "school" of single principle that unites the poets who have written in Montreal; nor is there any real sociological influence that we could not dispense with to produce this poetry. Its law is one of chance occurrence and of conditions favouring continuity, like a forest fire. It will no doubt continue for some time, perhaps to be fanned to a mighty blaze before "Canada's century" is over. But by that time—in fact, very soon—the Montreal movement will have to become a national movement, and more; as in fact it must do if it is to prove itself really successful, that is, a genuine new branch of English literature.

DIRECTION FOR CANADIAN POETS

LEO KENNEDY

1

Even though they have been frequently lionized by the leisured and philanthropic, English speaking Canadian poets have never been seriously accepted as interpreters of Canadian life. Perhaps that is because they have been con-

"Direction For Canadian Poets" by Leo Kennedy. From *New Frontier* I, (June, 1936), 21-4. Reprinted by permission of the author.

tent to function as interpreters of Canadian landscape. This easy preference sets its own penalty in the mediocre level which official Canadian poetry has reached at best.[1]

Today, in this sixth year of crisis and accelerated repression of civil liberties, the isolation of the Canadian poet from contemporary life is still taken for granted and accepted as an ideal, especially by the poet himself. In this time of impending war and incipient fascism, when the mode and standards of living of great numbers of middle class persons (from whose ranks Canadian poets hail) are being violently disrupted, our poets blithely comb their wooly wits for stanzas to clarify intimate, subjective reactions to Love, Beauty, the First Crocus, Snow in April and similar graceful but immediately irrelevant bubbles. In this they are abetted by what finds currency as Canadian "criticism." Here our professors of English Letters, commentators in the learned journals, and facile newspaper book reviewers are at fault. They have made no effort to locate Canadian poetry in its social place, and to see in its state of health or ill-health a register of the health or ill-health of Canadian society. Regrettably, our poetry is still regarded as an "art" which is to be attained for its own sake by a special cultivation of the senses.

It is the writer's contention that the time is now past for this kind of aesthetic flag-pole sitting. It is the purpose of this article to present the situation of our poets outlined above, out of the mouths of the poets themselves, and to suggest a direction to which their energies can be turned, with benefit to their own statures, and to a larger audience than they have ever before enjoyed. It is my thesis that the function of poetry is to interpret the contemporary scene faithfully; *to interpret especially the progressive forces in modern life which alone stand for cultural survival*. And it is my private recommendation that, setting theory aside, middle class poets had better hustle down from the twenty-fifth floor of their steam-heated janitor-serviced Ivory

---

[1]See the *Oxford Book of Canadian Verse* and allied desiderata.

Tower, and stand on the pavement and find out and take part in what is happening today, before the whole chaste edifice is blasted about their ears and laid waste!

2

There is a placid flatness to the run of Canadian poetry whether of 1882 or 1936 which invokes a smile of tolerance from the uninvolved observer, and makes the concerned participant—who looks for the work of adult minds—to squirm and suffer at so much documented obeisance to the namby-pamby. There is a hushed avoidance of self-criticism among the poets themselves, and a pious adherence to ideas and tricks of expression which have come to be identified with a tradition long since relegated to dust and archives. You have Jingo utterances from mental vacua; stereotyped descriptions of loons, lakes, pine trees, prairies and other natural Canadian phenomena; kindly and saccharine encomiums on fairies and dreams—especially dreams!—which might conceivably please children of tender and credulous years; apostrophied paeans in lame rhyming hexameters to Beauty, Life, Time, Love, Faith-hopeandcharity; smug and safe sonnets with an obvious clinch in their concluding couplets; ill-phrased effusions on Rembrandt portraits or Beethoven sonatas which daub their original subjects with a dreadful treacle.

In the matter of treatment, of rhyme and metre, official Canadian poetry remains the stamping ground of ante-deluvian formulae, of the second person singular, of e'er, o'er, yore, ye, of all the syllables clipped by the respected dead for metre's sake, and of all the consciously "poetical" words that enjoyed their day in Mrs. Hemans' youth. It is as though a colony of shoddy late-Tennysonian poets had been miraculously preserved here in all the drab bloom of their youth, cut from improving contact with the outer world, and reduced for purposes of criticism and comparison to the glib affabilities of their own numbers.

Canadian poetry has not at any time been of the first

or even the third water. No Walt Whitman sauntered on Montreal quays; no Poe fretted his life in a Toronto newspaper office. For generations Canadian poetry was the off-hour killcare of Empire Loyalist persons, who pursued their halt iambics and cornered their unresisting rhymes with all the zest of professional soul sleuths. Subsequently the domestic muse became paramour to a company of poets hailing from the east coast provinces, whose work was burdened with a prim Nordic consciousness and a second-hand Imperialism. The poetry of these well-meaning if limited individuals suffered from open-road infantilism in its later stages, as the work of Bliss Carman, Lampman, the Scotts and the several generations of Roberts bears glum witness. And the current crop of Canadian rhymers, with woefully few exceptions, has been prevented by its innate conservatism and imperviousness to the new, from swerving from the precedents laid down by the generation now mouldering under grass or in academic chairs.

Changes have taken place in modern English poetry; the United States has experienced a sequence of upheavals since the first crusading days of Harriet Monroe. In England and in the States those younger poets with anything to say have forced their way out of the back-water of the '20s. They have analysed the forces making for social disintegration, and have allied themselves with the progressive movement that offers freedom of function and hope of life. Reading Canadian poetry, you would hardly suspect this.

3

Consider the C.A.A.'s new *Canadian Poetry Magazine* and the various *Poetry Year Books* that preceded it. These official chapbooks offer a fair cross section of popular Canadian verse. Due to able and vigilant editorship, *Canadian Poetry Magazine* in its single quarterly issue published to date is years ahead of the old Year Books, but it is still full of sop. Basis and plan are sound: the editors publish and pay for the best poems they can get. They also award cash for the best poems in a given issue. But they do not get many good poems. They are not being written.

There are fifty-three poems in *Canadian Poetry Magazine* Vol. 1, No. 1. Two of them are written with a feeling for the times. The editors are to be congratulated on printing Livesay's *Day and Night,* a long, and for Canada, major poem about flesh and blood men working under inhuman factory conditions. Nat Benson's *Depression Chants* is the other contemporary poem.

Hark back three years to the *Poetry Year Book* of '32-'33, which editorially professes a sense of social responsibility. Warwick Chipman, poet and editor of the chapbook, is disturbed by the economic depression. I am also: I embrace him. His preface suggests in effect that poetry and the imagination that motivates poetry, may offer some palliative for the economic depression. He begins, "In these anxious days when people the world over are asking the same grim questions, and receiving the same bleak replies . . . when men have been betrayed in all their practical life; and, politically and economically, seem only to contrive their greater frustration . . . let imagination remind us of the immense reserves of the human soul.

"It is a hundred years since Goethe died, and Scott. The world they faced was as torn, as helpless, and as frightened as our own; and they replenished it and gave it strength. And today it may be that if we lack the will and vigour to follow the wisdom of a Salter or a Stamp, *some genius of imagination is on his way to give us the tone, the temper, and the fulness from which wisdom and will are restored.*

"Meanwhile our Seventh Year Book bears witness that the poets of this country continue undiminished and undismayed, remembering and reminding."

But let's look. The poems printed are announced to be the best of six hundred and fourteen submitted by three hundred poets from coast to coast. One observes that of the thirty-seven English poems, eight are preoccupied with God and Heaven in wistful, anticipatory terms. Others are

concerned with our old friend Beauty, Dawn, Optimism,
Gipsies and Blindness. A third group sticks to the fairies.
There is nothing here to help those "men who have been
betrayed in all their practical life," who, "politically and
economically, seem only to contrive their greater frustra-
tion." The poems have no bearing on experience. . . .

4

Now consider the published work of some Canadians who
do not regularly appear in local chapbooks. You quickly
observe that neo-metaphysical verse, so widely popularized
by T. S. Eliot, is still being ardently rewritten. Though
classicist Eliot has retired into Anglo-Catholicism, and his
leadership has been generally renounced, the apostolic
hand lies heavily on the verse of A. J. M. Smith and others.
Edith Sitwell, delicate, graceful as a glass crocus, and just
about as useful for the task now confronting Canadian
poets, is reflected in the work of Robert Finch. A. M.
Klein, doughty Zionist, is most praised for those poems in
which he displays his considerable Biblical knowledge, and
which re-create the ghetto history of European Jewry.
Bruce of Halifax writes convincingly of the sea and ships,
but his poetry carries the personal, insular emotion of one
still unaware of immediates. E. J. Pratt is latterly aware
in shorter poems of the deepening social crisis. Reclusive
Audrey Alexander Brown, whose curious personal history
has gone far to popularize her with Canadian readers, em-
ploys her undoubted talent in the manner and matter of
Keats and Swinburne. And the others are of an ilk. Only
Dorothy Livesay and F. R. Scott to date have quite shaken
themselves free of the superseded traditions, the former by
her study of marxist philosophy; the latter with pungent
satires on the more revered of our national institutions.[1]

A. J. M. Smith is easily the most talented and pains-
taking poet of all under consideration here. Yet the snob-
bery and obscurity of his work has for years restricted him

---

[1]See the files of the *Canadian Forum.*

to publication in those journals which hold sternly to aesthetics come hell and high water. He consistently vacillates from such hale stuff as:

NEWS OF THE PHOENIX[1]

They say the Phoenix is dying, some say dead—
Dead without issue is what one message said,
But that was soon suppressed, officially denied.

I think, myself, whoever sent it lied,
But the authorities were right to have him shot,
As a preliminary measure, whether he did or not.

to such surrealist exercise as NOCTAMBULE:[2]

Under the flag of this pneumatic moon,
—Blown up to bursting, whitewashed white
And clotted like the moon—the piracies of day
Scuttle the crank hulk of witless night.
The great black innocent Othello of a thing
Is undone by the nice clean pockethandkerchief
Of 6 a.m., and though the moon is only an old
Wetwash snotrag—horsemeat for good rosbif
Perhaps to utilise substitutes is what
The age has to teach us,
                              wherefor let the loud
Unmeaning warcry of treacherous daytime
Issue like whispers of love in the moonlight
—Poxy old cheat!

It seems the decent thing to line up sheep with sheep. My own single book of verse[3] reverts by way of Smith and Eliot to something of the matter of the metaphysicians. It is all about the fertility myth and rites of imitative magic that you find in Frazer's *Golden Bough,* in a Canadian dress. This preoccupation with abstractions of death and rebirth really resulted in a few poems of some sensibility. However, these are entirely subjective and lack contact with the larger reality.

---

[1]*New Verse*: December, 1933.
[2]*Rocking Horse*: Vol. 1, No. 3.
[3]*The Shrouding*: Macmillans in Canada.

NOW! All this sort of thing could get away with itself fifteen, ten, even five years ago. But not today. Canadian poets must assume adult responsibilities, if they are to survive as poets, let alone as people. Take language.

5

The language of our poetry is only too lifeless. Morley Callaghan suggested recently[1] that we develop our poetic forms out of the richness and imagery of Canadian speech. He is entirely right: they can develop no other way. John Howard Lawson adds: "The only speech which lacks colour is that of people who have nothing to say. People whose contact with reality is direct and varied must create a mode of speech which expresses that contact."[2]

Poetry cannot be both a living thing and an archaeological exercise. "The poet who, using an obsolete technique, attempts to express his whole conception is compelled . . . to be content with slovenly thought and feeling . . . [he] cannot expect to write well unless he is abreast of his times, honest with himself, and uses a technique sufficiently flexible to express precisely those subtleties of thought and feeling in which he differs from his predecessors."[3]

This much is clear: poetry not of the living scene cannot be genuine because of the artificiality and self-consciousness that writes itself in. Poetry that is of it, cannot worry along with the old forms, because they do not fit. The progressive young poets of the United States and Day Lewis, Spender, Thomas and others in England know about this. We must too.

What phases of the living scene shall Canadian poets write about? *Any—so long as they are genuinely experienced and understood by the poet.* Because I have called attention to poems of factory life by Klein and Livesay, it may be felt that this article invites everyone to write them.

---

[1] *Maclean's* Magazine: February, 1936.
[2] *Theory and Technique of Playwriting*: Putnam.
[3] Michael Roberts: preface to *New Signatures*: Hogath.

Nothing of the kind! Industrial poems cannot be written by middle class poets who have no contact with the subject. The poet whose livelihood is still intact may have trouble conjuring a communicable emotion and indignation out of fifty shabby, unshaven men in a breadline . . . until he has thought the whole thing through and realized that breadlines in a wheat country are illogical and criminal, and that he and his kind may be only some steps removed from a like condition. He must touch life at a thousand points . . . grasp the heroism, joy and terror, the courage under privation and repression, the teeming life-stuff all round him that is also the stuff of great poetry! Poetry that is real, Canadian and contemporary can be written to-morrow by poets who worried about "dreams" and their precious egos yesterday. It will be welcomed by millions of Canadians who want their children to grow up straight-limbed to enjoy a heritage of prosperity and peace, and who want the kind of writing that will help bring this about.

We need poetry that reflects the lives of our people, working, loving, fighting, groping for clarity. We need satire—fierce, scorching, aimed at the abuses which are destroying our culture and which threaten life itself. Our poets have lacked direction for their talents and energies in the past—I suggest that today it lies right before them.

2. Leo Kennedy

LEO KENNEDY AND THE RESURRECTION OF CANADIAN POETRY

W. E. COLLIN

No one who has followed the articles on Canadian poets recently appearing in *The Canadian Forum* can be in any doubt about the feelings our young poets entertain towards their predecessors. L. A. MacKay rejects Carman as American and favours Pratt, Livesay, and Klein; and now Leo Kennedy, writing of another immortal, Archibald Lampman, says that "the current generation of Canadian poets . . . has chucked him out, neck, crop, and rhyming dictionary." As the year proceeds the other idols of the past will undoubtedly be brought to dust by the blasts of these iconoclasts of whom Kennedy, I think, is the most passionately destructive.

Kennedy has had many ups and downs. He was born in Liverpool twenty-five years ago and came to Canada when he was five. His family was not literary, and what books were found in the house were brought in by Kennedy who, for seven years, served as a shipping clerk and bookkeeper in his father's ship-chandler's business. I have heard that as a youngster he cleared off to sea and spent four months peeling potatoes and washing dishes on a C.P.R. tramp among West Indian ports.

His literary adventures began with his meeting the men who ran *The McGill Fortnightly Review* (1926-1928):

"Leo Kennedy and the Resurrection of Canadian Poetry" by W. E. Collin. From *Canadian Forum*, XIV (October 1933), 24-7. Copyright 1933 by *Canadian Forum*. Reprinted by permission of W. E. Collin and *Canadian Forum*.

F. R. Scott, A. J. M. Smith, Alan Latham, and Leon Edel. When the *Fortnightly* ceased, *The Canadian Mercury* was launched, and continued through six numbers, from December, 1928, to June, 1929; Kennedy was associated with Jean Burton, F. R. Scott, and Felix Walter on the editorial board. And when the *Mercury* closed its doors the subscribers' list was taken over by *The Canadian Forum* which has since published much of the work of the Montreal writers: Felix Walter is an associate editor.

A little later than the founding of *The Canadian Mercury* Kennedy went to New York and married a Jewess. In many ways the New York experience was a wretched one. Kennedy was a reporter for *The World*, reviewed for *The Bookman, The Commonweal, The Herald Tribune* and a little journal published by the E. P. Dutton Company. He also brought his book-keeping into service. Then, during the consternation caused by the breaking of the stock market, they returned to Montreal.

It is obvious that Kennedy has been more concerned with living than with studying. He is an emotional, not a learned man: and his emotions make his anatomy quiver and jerk. He was born to translate those emotions into their artistic verbal equivalents. And, however much he may be pre-occupied with the metaphysical poets and their twentieth-century representatives, he is unfitted to write criticism in any way comparable to T. S. Eliot's or poetry like Klein's: nor are his critics likely to place his poems in parallel series with Paul Valery's, for the simple reason that he has no metaphysics. Kennedy does not start with philosophical concepts as a basis for his poetry. That has saved him from falling into errors of allusionism and conceptism. His poetry may show an early indulgence in Elinor Wylie ("Reproach to Myself," "Martha and Mary," and the close, smooth grain of his sonnets), and T. S. Eliot ("Rite of Spring" and the sickly "Litany of Our Time"), but he feels life intensely enough to be able to nourish his own language without recourse at every turn to the old

masters. He can recite pages of Eliot, but if he ever imi-
tates such lost words as:

> If the lost word is lost, if the spent word is spent,
> If the unheard, unspoken
> Word is unspoken, unheard . . .

he is lost. Take John Donne and Saint John out of those
lines and let the evening breezes blow away the downy
seeded milkweed.

We have no immediate cause for fear. Kennedy has been
trying to find life and to find himself; prospecting for a
metal fine enough to surrender itself wholly to the impress
of his emotions; searching for the Word and the Myth
which would be the perfect literary vehicle of his sensi-
bility. He is very fortunate to have found these things;
they will permit him to unfold his dimensions and reveal
his greatness.

Of the contributors to *The Canadian Mercury*, A. J. M.
Smith, especially, was inclined to metaphysical poetry and
had something to convey to Kennedy: a dissatisfaction
with lyrical poetry, and interest in Eliot. But Kennedy, I
think, owes more to Eliot: readings in seventeenth-century
literature and directions for finding the Myth.

Ten years ago Eliot observed that we object to "the
simplification and separation of the mental faculties" and
opined that "one of the characteristics of Donne which
wins him . . . his interest for the present age is his fidelity
to emotion as he finds it."[1] Precisely the same feelings are
behind Kennedy's censure of Lampman: "For all his care-
ful observation, little in the form of an emotional climax
comes out of it."[2] But in poetry, crude emotional conflicts
may give us no more esthetic satisfaction than photo-
graphic descriptions. Kennedy's reading has touched his
emotions in a very important way. In *The Golden Bough*
he discovered the Myth. The Myth permeated, became
one substance with his Emotion and engendered all his

[1] *The Nation and the Athenaeum*, June 9th, 1923.
[2] *The Canadian Forum*, May, 1933.

poems; which are the living figures of his unified sensibility—a rare possession that present-day critics have lauded in Donne and the others.

*   *   *

> Webster was much possessed by death
> And saw the skull beneath the skin
>
> Donne, I suppose, was another.
>
> *T. S. Eliot*

Along a street in Verdun, Montreal, there is a Funeral Home, easily visible by day and illuminated by night. Donne in his shroud was not nearer death than Kennedy as he listened to the mortician's details of a modern embalming:

When washing a body, padding a cheek, or clearing the entrails out of some blue abdomen, Caleb's fingers deftly danced.

> "Death comes for the Undertaker."
> Arrange their waxen limbs with care.
>
> Lid the flat staring eye, as pale as ice;
> Bind up the fallen jaw; then fold the palms
> Decorously upon the breast.
>
> the oaken coffin and the pall . . .
> The rented purple hangings in the hall
> Over the torn wallpaper . . . and the frail
> Blossoms of candles sepulchrally pale.

It may appear on a first reading that Kennedy moves between the Funeral Home and the Cemetery; that he has built his poetic on a passage from Sir Thomas Browne: "Now since these dead bones have already outlasted the living ones of Methuselah . . . what Prince can promise such diuturnity unto his relics, or might not glady say:

> "Sic ego componi versus in ossa velim."[1]

---

[1] *Hydriotaphia*, or Urn Burial.

That is no more than a surface impression. He is faithful to "emotion as he finds it"; but he has used his experience and emotions as primitive peoples used imitative magic, to revive life in the ground: as a poet he has graced the gruesome paraphernalia of death and burial in Montreal with the anemones of the Syrian Adonis:

> Weep not for Adonais . . . .

In that way he has made us look upon present life as a continuation of the past history of the race; he has enriched human experience by "widening the domain of reality," as Eliot would say.

Living in a country once inhabited by Indians, Kennedy might reasonably have connected our funeral rites with the ceremonial of death among the Algonquins and Iroquois. But the place was not as powerful an influence as the moment. Kennedy grew up in the relaxing atmosphere which settled upon our Waste Land after the war and, following Eliot's lead, he discovered new gods: Attis, Osiris, and Adonis. In *The Golden Bough* he read that the annual ceremony of the death and resurrection of Adonis was a dramatic representation of the decay and revival of plant life; and that the Easter celebration of the dead and risen Christ may have been "grafted upon a similar celebration of the dead and risen Adonis . . . celebrated in Syria at the same season." That was the link that Kennedy wanted, for out of the scuttling of his Catholicism, the thing that he had cherished and preserved was the Easter Cycle (Life-Death-Life); the most amazing thing to him. So it is that the Myth has fertilized his Canadian sensibility, made it bring forth solemnly beautiful and strangely moving poems:

> April is no month for burials.
>
> Blood root and trillium break out of cover.
>
> Where sapling boys and girls are sweetly aching
> For willow sprouts, and the smell of fresh earth breaking
>
> And girls now seedlings in their father's reins.

In all countries, I suppose, from time beyond record, Spring Songs have been sung and Spring Rites celebrated —even in Canada before the Puritan and Victorian occupation. Why was Lampman, who leaned upon the Mighty Mother, so insensible to the flow of sap under the maple bark and in his own organs? He revolted against the Church yet he was not vigorous enough to wean himself from an effete poetic tradition. We have privately admired him for a few stylistic powers which he possessed and made little use of; in our hearts we have reproached him for not humanly fertilizing Canadian nature. There were celebrated anthropologists in his day; but Tylor, occupied largely in discussing animism, a religion of spirits rather than One Spirit, did not present to Lampman a glorified Figure of the Resurrection. Lampman needed a Myth. We are dissatisfied with his Aprils and Octobers after reading Kennedy's "Epithalamium before Frost" and:

WORDS FOR A RESURRECTION

> Each pale Christ stirring underground
> Splits the brown casket of its root,
> Wherefrom the rousing soil upthrusts
> A narrow, pointed shoot . . .
>
> And bones long quiet under frost
> Rejoice as bells precipitate
> The loud, ecstatic sundering,
> The hour inviolate.
>
> This Man of April walks again . . .
> Such marvel does the time allow . . .
> With laughter in His blessed bones,
> And lilies on His brow.

This Man of April walks again!

Of all the descriptions of resurrected gods, as Adonis spirit of the corn; of all the descriptive phrases that Fray Luis de Leon meditated upon in *De los Nombres de Cristo* none, I feel, has more power to move our imaginations than that; except Christ's own: I am the Bread of

Life. We may take that little poem apart, unweave the ideas and references, open our hearts to the emotion, and then read it over again to marvel at its subtle perfection. I know of no Canadian poem in which there is such absolute and beautiful blending of thought and feeling, such amazing unity of being.

This young poet, as Adonis, as Christ, dies in order to live. He dramatizes death in order to reveal a sequel: perennial resurrection. He faces corruption and dissolution in order to magnify the immortality of beauty. Job's words are his: "I have said to corruption, Thou art my father: to the worm, Thou art my mother and my sister." But he has espoused Death in order to cry Epithalamium! The paradox is a discovery of startling poetic power:

> Now shall I cry Epithalamium!

—even while the sap is retreating before the pricking frost!

The title "Epithalamium" in Donne suggested to Kennedy names for some of his poems. This one he first called "Sequel":

EPITHALAMIUM

This body of my mother, pierced by me,
In grim fulfilment of our destiny,
Now dry and quiet as her fallow womb
Is laid beside the shell of that bridegroom
My father, who with eyes towards the wall
Sleeps evenly; his dust stirs not at all,
No syllable of greeting curls his lips,
As to that shrunken side his leman slips.

Lo! these are two of unabated worth
Who in the shallow bridal bed of earth
Find youth's fecundity, and of their swift
Comminglement of bone and sinew, lift
—A lover's seasonable gift to blood
Made bitter by a parched widowhood—
This bloom of tansy from the fertile ground:
My sister, heralded by no moan, no sound.

In the old Semitic myths the reproductive energies of nature were personified as male and female; water was especially identified with the one power and earth with the other. In Kennedy the soil is a matrix; "pools of melted snow," "water slurring underground" we may consider the sperm and promise of future life. Spring shoots will pierce the matrix of the soil: then we may lay the crocuses, hyacinths, ragweed and lilac leaves upon our sorrowing hearts and bind the April grass about our brows. The mad Pope Hadrian fled to his villa to grow blooms:

> He found such pleasure in the roots of things
> That plot a resurrection out of sight.

Kennedy moves the idea of resurrection from place to place with intent to dramatize the revelation. He finds a Hamlet sinking "beneath the treason of his esteemed flesh"; a philosopher moving unwillingly into the "still repository of his dust"; a widow sitting over her dead husband thinking of Christ's "Come forth Lazarus" . . . and hearing only "the rattling of a hearse"; a recluse "wry and arid in her soul" poisoning herself and quickly realizing that "life was the precious gift." He finds occasion to write his own epitaph:

> SELF EPITAPH
> TO BE CARVED IN SALT
>
> His heart was brittle;
> His wits were scattered;
> He wrote of dying
> As though life mattered.

A pleasing subtlety of conception in "Exile endured," one of his chaste and melodious sonnets, is due to the marriage of his Emotion with the Vegetation Myth:

> I . . . .
> Who have grown harsh and arid under stone
> That shrivels up the heart, and splits the bone!

"Daughter of Leda," without the Myth would be a Pre-Raphaelite exercise. The Myth has engendered life in the foil of his poetry:

> Afix with gummy maple sap
> The tear that widens at each thrust
> Of ragweed straining from the dust.

> For all the beauty winter cannot kill.

> gaunt unresurrected sons of God,
> Crocus bulbs parched and patient under sod.

> the drip
> Of snow water through the dark.

The Myth swells his lines with so much meaning:

> Bind up this heart that splits and bleeds.

> . . . I pass
> Among bleached bones of summer.

Kennedy's poetry is not a game played by a cold brain organized in this or that fashion but a soul's experience, ardent and alive, breathed into harmonious rhythms and rolling chants—the music of a harmonized sensibility. His long lines (which invite comparison with those of Archibald MacLeish) have the power and solemnity of a great drama:

> Gather the fringes of earth, then draw together
> The parts of this brown wound, and bind them fast
> With measured stitches of your spade, Gravedigger.

> Eyes misted with passion, the lids heavily aswoon,
> The nails bruising the palms in ecstasy . . .
> The long shuddering breath, and the ensuing quiet.

> And weep and curse and smash your heart to bits.

As he found life in death, so he has searched for words which, though old and decaying, have a quick potency in their dry roots; Saxon words (here again we think of

MacLeish) taking us back beyond the Elizabethans to the beginnings of our poetry: leman, charily, cleave, rime:

> How shall I cleave me from my works?

He has found the Word, as he found the Myth, and entered into the vital being of it to make it his. The reader is conscious of this reintegration in his best stories (for example, "A Priest in the Family"[1]) and in every line of his poetry:

> Now that leaves shudder from the hazel limb,
> And poppies pod, and maples whirl their seed.
>
> And rime surmised at morning pricks the rim
> Of tawny stubble, husk and perishing weed.
>
> And the first crocus hoists its yellow crest!

Nature's periods thrust themselves into our lives in Canada more violently than in other countries and we scorn them at our peril. Yet what Prince among us has promised diuturnity to his relics by turning his emotions outward among those eternal processes? Vanity, says the Preacher:

> All these things endured their time and are broken,

says the Poet, too—that he might hail the Resurrection! The Triumph of Life is a trivial word until it illumines the darkness of our flesh.

A new Myth had to blow over our frost-bound Canadian fields that a new Poet might marvel at the miracle of "water slurring underground" and chant the unfailing quickening of Beauty and Love.

> He shall grow up . . . as a tender plant, and as root out
> of a dry ground.

[1]*The Canadian Forum*, April, 1933.

THE BUSHEL OF PLATITUDE

HAROLD ROSENBERG

No doubt there was once, and perhaps it still exists somewhere, a kind of life which Mr. Kennedy's verses about Death and the Earth might adorn. Yet, though he inscribes his book with quotations, yesterday fashionable, from Webster and T. S. Eliot, it is hard to say that he has really kept going.

Most visibly, it is a question of words, the exact register of a literary mind's incisiveness or lethargy. And Mr. Kennedy, approaching the grave with verbal implements like these:

> A brute insensate as the harrowed clod,

and

> The cloistered ease of those interred hereunder,

ought not to be surprised if he turns up nothing but a corpse.

It is almost in the nature of an obligation to the best poetry and criticism of our time that we do not accept this too calmly. The little mannerisms, cuteness, and looking-glass skirmishes of an old-maid vocabulary can do enough damage in their place. What was Mr. Kennedy doing while he was reading Webster and Eliot?

> His voice is silent; his lips are cold;
> And Death has anointed his eyes with mould.

Platitudes are inescapable; and, as the most persevering human products we know of, they should be reckoned with by poetry. But besides the difference that exists between

"The Bushel of Platitude" (a review of *The Shrouding* by Leo Kennedy) by Harold Rosenberg. From *Poetry*, XLIV (September 1934), 345-7. Copyright 1934 by The Modern Poetry Association. Reprinted by permission of Harold Rosenberg and the Editor of *Poetry*.

the handling of a platitude by a poet and the manipulation of a poet by a platitude, there is also a difference in kinds of platitude. In Mr. Kennedy's verses, Paris has been slain, Helen stands on the walls of Troy, and Lazarus prepares for his habeas corpus from the tomb—but those events happened only this morning in comparison with the state of preservation of the following rhetoric:

> Wilted and grey, the lily heads decline
> And spread a rank miasmic scent, until
> Corruption spawns upon the shallow hill—

and so on.

NEW NOTES IN CANADIAN POETRY

E. J. PRATT

To those who are studying the character of Canadian literature it must be a matter of deep interest to follow the developments which have taken place in poetry during the last four or five years. It is not too much to claim that we are witnessing a Renaissance in the genuine sense of the term—a birth whose paternity cannot be laid at the door of any literary progenitor in this country but will show blood stains with the lusty foundlings exercising their Anglo-Saxon (and other) lungs in England and the United States.

This movement exhibits a general divergence from the main Canadian stream with its nature photography and diluted transcendentalism. It is, however, traditional and contemporary in the sense in which the modernism of writers like Eliot, Pound, MacLeish and Jeffers can blend

"New Notes in Canadian Poetry" by E. J. Pratt. From *Canadian Comment*, (February 1934), 26-7. Reprinted by permission of the Estate of E. J. Pratt.

with the work of Donne, Sir Thomas Browne and the metaphysical poets down to Emily Dickinson.

The vital centre of this energy is in Montreal. Most of the work has appeared only in magazines, but it is attracting wide attention for its originality, its strength, and its constant reflection of the ferments and moods which are stirring the emotional life of the world today. It has all the spirit of adventure, the zest of being in the intellectual and artistic advance of the age. We shall do well to watch the later and systematic production of the group composed in part of F. R. Scott, A. J. M. Smith, Abraham Klein and Leo Kennedy.

The first contribution in volume form is by Kennedy— *The Shrouding* (Macmillan), a slim modest collection indeed but of sterling poetic content, utterly unlike anything in our Canadian output up-to-date, and, considering that the author is only in his middle twenties, one might reasonably expect that the years ahead of him possess major fulfilments. It is not often that a first presentation displays such finished craftsmanship and a technical manner which force interlinear meanings of a deep emotional cast upon condensed expression. "The Gravedigger's Rhapsody" reveals a command of strong undulating rhythm with an ability to sustain the purity of the organizing idea in the midst of material which, at first sight, may not appear to contain much malleability. Indeed, the impression which remains after the reading of the poems is that of triumph over refractory content. The sense of the unusual sometimes springs out of the novelty of the subject or out of the freshness of the attack on familiar themes. Individual lines and phrases flash out on every page, indicating that Kennedy rarely suffers from the malaise of the majority of our younger poets—the acceptance of clichés, worn-out counters of expression which furnish the line of least resistance when inspiration is at a low ebb.

I think I may be anticipating one criticism of this volume when I point out—what the author himself would probably acknowledge—that the general emotional attitude towards life does not find sufficient relief or variety. The autumnal tones are consistently present though they are always impressive. This quality, however, distinguishes most of the characteristic poetry of the age, and one would expect to find a measure of it in any writer who is attempting to subject the world as it now exists to an honest analysis. What is more important is that whatever viewpoint is taken should be stated with conviction and sincerity and, I am sure, that these poems attest the reality of the signature.

I do not find it easy to offer clipped examples of his power of poetic phrasing for, apart from the present limitation of space, the quotations would not contribute the full value shared by the context and, moreover, an outstanding characteristic of his poetry is the cumulative appeal built up by masses of realistic detail. The imagery is so largely processional.

The final critical result is not simply an estimate of a poetic accomplishment. This in itself is considerable, I am convinced. It is rather the feeling of promise of what is to appear in future work. But enough of the ore has been sampled in this verse to indicate richness and depth. I should like to quote in their entirety such profoundly moving poems as "Rite of Spring," "Prophecy for Icarus," "Reproach to Myself," and "Quatrains against Grief." But there is space for only one:

WORDS FOR A RESURRECTION

Each pale Christ stirring underground
Splits the brown casket of its root,
Wherefrom the rousing soil upthrusts
A narrow, pointed shoot. . . .

And bones long quiet under frost
Rejoice as bells precipitate
The loud, ecstatic sundering,
The hour inviolate.

This Man of April walks again . . .
Such marvel does the time allow . . .
With laughter in His blessed bones,
And lilies on His brow.

LEO KENNEDY'S POETRY

PETER STEVENS

Kennedy was associated with the Montreal poets, and his
work had bccn particularly influenced by A. J. M. Smith's
pronouncements about Eliot and the Metaphysicals.
Kennedy went further in his use of Metaphysical modes
than any other of the Montreal group. He deliberately
used some archaic language as well as subject-matter deriv-
ing from Jacobean literature, particularly later Jacobean
drama with its insistence on man's mortality and transi-
tory stay on earth. Kennedy was not altogether successful
in assimilating the language and the modes of the Meta-
physicals, with the result that the language too often draws
attention to itself as being archaic. There is little varia-
tion of tone in the volume so that his constant emphasis
on death tends to strike the reader as either an indulgence
in morbidity for its own sake or an unwitting exaggera-
tion. Nonetheless, Kennedy's verse has some interest in
that it was a deliberate attempt to write a poetry without
any real reference to the Canadian scene, a deliberate
shunning of national feeling, a kind of verse not attempted
by any other Canadian, although Kennedy himself was to

"Leo Kennedy's Poetry" by Peter Stevens. From *The Development
of Canadian Poetry Between the Wars and Its Reflection of Social
Awareness*, an unpublished Ph.D. Thesis, University of Saskatchewan,
Saskatoon, 148-155 and 229-237. Copyright 1968 by the author and
the University of Saskatchewan. Reprinted by permission of the Uni-
versity of Saskatchewan and the author. The pages reprinted here are
only parts of Chapters V and VII of the thesis.

reject *The Shrouding* later on. It is also an interesting volume in the sense that Kennedy's verse was almost wholly lacking in the modern spirit. Both Scott and Smith used the Metaphysical impulse in their verse, but it was filtered through a modern consciousness in both feeling and form. This cannot be said about Kennedy's verse. It shows no concession to "modern" concerns about form; the language is, even when it is not archaic, almost standard "poetic" language (in the sense that he does not use colloquialisms or even up-to-date movement of language). The opening poem of the volume, "Epithalamium," sets the tone and will serve as an illustration of the strengths and weaknesses of Kennedy's poetry. The first stanza reads:

> This body of my mother, pierced by me,
> In grim fulfilment of our destiny,
> Now dry and quiet as her fallow womb
> Is laid beside the shell of that bridegroom
> My father, who with eyes towards the wall
> Sleeps evenly; his dust stirs not at all,
> No syllable of greeting curls his lips,
> As to that shrunken side his leman slips.

In general, the paradox of the title in relation to death is well worked out in this stanza, but some of the details seem exaggerated or too emphatic—the use of "this" and "that" seems unnecessary, for "that bridegroom" and "that shrunken side" do not need emphasizing. The second line is rather vague: what is the "destiny," the simple relationship of mother and son? "Curls" brings a suggestion of sneering, surely not intended in this context. "Leman" is too archaic and in a sense leaves the reader outside the poem, seeing it rather as a fanciful idea rather than a deeply-felt and realized statement in verse. The poem continues:

> Lo! these are two of unabated worth,
> Who in the shallow bridal bed of earth

Find youth's fecundity, and of their swift
Comminglement of bone and sinew, lift
—A lover's seasonable gift to blood
Made bitter by a parched widowhood—
This bloom of tansy from the fertile ground:
My sister, heralded by no moan, no sound.

This stanza starts badly with "Lo!" (Kennedy changed this word to "Yet" when he reprinted the poem in *New Provinces*.) Nor is it apparent why their worth is "unabated." Does he mean it is unabated in his memory? The details about "dust" and "shrunken," the insistence on the bodily functions of love and birth tend to negate the idea of some worth beyond life experienced through the body. But again the paradox is well expressed in the following three lines. The parenthesis is uncertain in its tone—why is the gift "seasonable"? Is it the season of death or is it the season of spring? Perhaps this is to be taken in this uncertain way as part of the paradox, for the "bloom of tansy" refers to the idea of wedding-death, birth-death, and life arising from death together. Tansy is a bitter aromatic plant used as a flavouring in a cake eaten at Easter. Thus, the tansy, a small insignificant flower, is born into the world with "no moan, no sound," perhaps making no effect on the world and yet also being born easily into the world, a symbol perhaps of a life beyond man's pain and mortality.

Sometimes Kennedy's poetry is spoilt by a too close identification with other poets. Echoes of Eliot stand in the way of a poem's statement; the phrases obtrude themselves too much. "Rite of Spring" opens with "April is no month for burials," and this allusion to the opening of "The Waste Land" seems too overt. In some poems there are echoes of "Ash Wednesday," and one poem, "Mendelian Theory," is a composite of many Elizabethan lyrics with phrases echoing in one's mind, bothering the reader

with references to other poems without adding anything
to Kennedy's own poem:

> Being of clay compounded, and of air
> That is a common element enough,
> I am, by virtue of the flesh I wear,
> A man of coarse yet serviceable stuff
> Fit to beget a burgher or a thief—
> A new Caligula or a priest of God—
> Some Shelley with dogmatic unbelief—
> A brute insensate as the harrowed clod.

In reading lines such as these, one tends to agree with
Harold Rosenberg's summary of Kennedy's book, "the
little mannerisms, cutenesses, and looking-glass skirmishes
of an old-maid vocabulary."[1] And yet at times Kennedy
achieves a sound pastiche of Elizabethan lyricism as in
"Mirror For Lovers" and in "Mad Boy's Song" unspoilt
by archaic language and using images as embodiments of
madness:

> The small activity of mice,
> The velvet passing of a moth,
> And one grey spider's cautious tread
> Make thunder in this shed:
> Where God has stored his tightened drum—
> A mind inside a head!

Three or four long meditations on man's mortality are
unrelieved by any kind of humour or by simple serious-
ness. The attitudes to death seem assumed rather than real.
The best of these is a poem about a suicide, "Exeunt
Without Sennet," for sections of this poem have some
effective simplicity of description. But his range of feeling
is altogether too narrow, and the insistence on death over-
powers any real thoughts of resurrection, apart from one
or two poems. W. E. Collin over-emphasizes the ideas of
resurrection in Kennedy's poetry; he calls Kennedy "this

---

[1]*Poetry*, September, 1934, p. 346.

man of April," a phrase taken from one of Kennedy's poems. The poetry does not live up to the idea expressed in his "Self-Epitaph":

> He wrote of dying
> As though life mattered.

Occasionally, particularly in some epitaphs, a kind of bleak humour lightens the tone:

> Fat Edward Topergut sprawls here,
> Whose coffin, large as tun of beer,
> Took six men's stubborn brawn and heft;
> A thimbleful of dust is left.

Sometimes, images seem to fulfil the imagists' demand for economy and summary of a complex of emotions in a single instant, although Kennedy's cast of mind seems too rhetorical to allow the images to stand on their own. However, one can lift some images out of context and present them as evidence, perhaps, that Kenndy had taken notice of imagist principles:

> And now the geese are flown, and now the river
>   Is low, and on its banks brown nettles stand
> Rasping their shrivelled, needy stalks together

> Sand shifts with every tide, and gravel
> Slurs against the rock

> Blackbirds would gabble where the larches throw
> Fantastic shadows on deep moving pools
> Of yellow sunlight

The last section of the volume is entitled "Outcry On The Time," suggesting that Kennedy was already thinking that his poetry should be more firmly rooted in the world around him. This, indeed, was the direction his poetry and his ideas about poetry were to take after the publication of *The Shrouding*. Yet his poems in this section continue in the same mode as the other sections, the comments on his own position in his own time being generalized and vague:

> If I speak charily of wheeling gulls,
> And coast winds blowing freshly at low tide,
> It is because a sea-bred fit annuls
> My sober preference for this safe hearthside;
> And if with glib lip service I abjure
> The bobbing hulls of dories in the cove,
> It is because my peace is insecure,
> Assailed by everything I truly love.
>
> I am reminded how the rain's tooth gnaws
> Through oaken planks of hulks along the beach;
> I am waylaid at every turn and pause
> By muttering of water out of reach;
> And taste, as ghostly mews wing strongly south
> Salt in the heart, and sand against the mouth.

Here a generalized landscape is used as a means to imply all is not well in the state of society; but the poem also implies that nothing can be done, however strongly the poet feels. After reading through the volume and coming to this poem, in spite of its good closing line, the reader tends to take it as just another expression of man's insignificance in the face of greater forces, not as an "outcry on the time." In some ways, Kennedy is using the technique of the younger English poets of the 1930s, most notably W. H. Auden and C. Day Lewis, a technique expressing social dissatisfaction in terms of landscape and the seasons. The difference between these poets and Kennedy is that the English poets were much more positive; their outcry at least had the virtue of looking to some optimistic future, a virtue which events proved soon to be an illusion, but this attitude rose above gloom and morbidity and on occasions produced sound poetry, at times even good poetry and generally better "outcries on the time" than Kennedy's, as in these examples, for instance, from a generally unsatisfactory poem by C. Day Lewis:

But winter still rides rough-shod upon us,
Summer comes not for wishing nor warmth at will:
Passes are blocked and glaciers pen us
Round the hearth huddled, hoping for a break,
Playing at patience, reporting ill.
Aware of changed temperature one shall wake
And rushing to window arouse companions
To feel frost surrender, an ice age finished;

and

> Though winter's barricade delays,
> Another season's in the air;
> We'll sow the spring in our young days,
> Found a Virginia everywhere.
>
> Look where the ranks of crocuses
> Their rebel colours will display
> Coming with quick fire to redress
> The balance of a wintry day.
>
> Those daffodils that from the mould
> Drawing a sweet breath soon shall flower,
> With a year's labour get their gold
> To spend it on a sunny hour.

Kennedy was to become more positive in his attitudes to his own poetry and to the poetry of his contemporaries, as we shall see later, but his outcry on the time in *The Shrouding* is too closely related to the other poems in the volume to rise above their mannerisms and poses. The insistence on death through the volume is so strong that it smacks of poetic posture rather than of genuine feeling, apart from a few poems, and as the poems of outcry at the end repeat the same images and methods, the protest also seems a posture of defiance rather than a deeply felt emotion. However jejune and naive the feelings of Day Lewis and the other English poets appear now, there is no doubt that they were genuine at the time the poems were written. Kennedy's "Litany For These Days" carries connotations over from the earlier funereal sections:

> Lily of the marshes, rooted in mire and slime,
> Drab-petalled, musk-scented, lapped by no tide,
> Virgin polluted, emblem of death in life,
> Flower with miasmic breath,
> Mottled flower of decay,
> Flower enshrined in corruption,
> Flower latticed by dry reeds,
> Blooming in secret, fated to rot obscurely. . .
>
> Pray for us, o most foetid blossom.
> Pray for our souls, spiritless as thy marshes,
> Pray for our virtue, stagnant as thy waters,
> Pray for our sins, lifeless as thy sap.

As can be seen from "Directions For Canadian Poets," Leo Kennedy made a great plea to Canadian poets to tackle the political situation of their time, yet he rejected Smith's poetry probably because Smith's political poetry could not be reduced to his simplistic formula. In October, 1934 he published a poem in *Canadian Forum* which, although it used the same imagery as his early poems, was in fact a rejection of those poems. The poem was an attack on those

> Who venerate the mildewed coffin plank;
> Quote epitaphs in sleep, and don the shroud;
> Eschew sweet air and cultivate the dank
> Breath of the charnel in a foetid cloud.

Such morbid people, the poem went on to state rather hysterically, should be ruthlessly attacked:

> Let crows descend, then may they be assailed
> By glittering beaks that tear and maim and fetch
>
> The eye-ball from its socket like a grape,
> The blistered tongue from out the fallen jaws;

Yet Kennedy's own poetic method tended to romanticize to some extent the images of violence, the kind of romanticizing that was to crop up a little later in his political poetry:

> Let moles assemble from their corridors,
>   And burrowing the skin, prise out the bone
> To suck the marrow; may their velvet jaws
>   Polish the skull to lustre of a stone.

Nonetheless, Kennedy's was a genuine concern for the real purpose of poetry in Canada in the 1930s and it was an act of poetic faith to reject his earlier poetry in order to search for a more immediate poetry. He published some poems in *New Frontier* under his own name and under the pseudonyms of Arthur Beaton and Leonard Bullen.[1] His aims and methods might be best approached by looking at "New Comrade" (September, 1936), a poem similar in subject-matter to Smith's "Son-and-Heir." Kennedy's prediction for the child's future is a new era brought about by revolution, and he places a picture of the new-born child in sharp juxtaposition to pictures of the revolutionary process:

> he is small yet for the discipline and the mass action
> young for the fiery speeches and the blind police violence
> puckered and wailing
>   he is new and unused to a dying
>   world
> early for barricades

This juxtaposition continues in the picture of the baby described in terms of a political salute—an idea brought into the reader's mind by Kennedy's salutation:

> Gravely we salute him
> comrade with the creased fist thrown back on the pillow

The visions of the future in this poem are not pictures of bourgeois wealth as in Smith's poem but rather images of scientific achievements perhaps to be reached by the new

---

[1]This information is given in F. W. Watt's unpublished Ph.D. thesis, *Radicalism in English-Canadian Literature Since Confederation*, University of Toronto, 1957.

comrade; but this future is still to be conditioned by the revolutionary process. Thus again Kennedy uses juxtaposition of images to make his point; the new comrade may grow up to

> span an ocean with steel
> > fetter the atom
> or split like a ripe fruit in the enfilade of dum-dums.

So far the poem has concentrated on detail without drifting into vague political moralizing. The method of juxtaposition is repeated by implication later in the poem, when Kennedy summarizes the revolutionary intentions of the present generation. People in this generation (as opposed to the generation the new comrade will grow up with) are

> painfully unlearning error
> > yielding
> confusion for freedom inchmeal with difficult labour.

Note here that images of growing and birth are related to the political message of the poem and when these images revert to the new child, they carry these political implications with them:

> We welcome this comrade gravely (initiate
> in a harsh time
> > fearful of noise and falling
> stung to grimace by strangeness of shape and movement
> startled by daylight.

The poem closes with a prayer:

> may he inherit the earth
> > the fruit of our passion
> the life sweetness after the bullet spent
> may he have peace and work creation where our shadows
> > > are.

This is a somewhat weak ending to a poem which has attempted by means of juxtaposition and a simple pattern of images (even the close echoes the image of "ripe fruit" earlier in the poem) to give expression to the general concept of revolutionary optimism, the hope for the future in the midst of poverty, corruption and political apathy and betrayal. Yet it is hardly the "immediate" poetry that Kennedy demanded from other Canadian poets.

Kennedy was very much aware of the general situation of life as well as of poetry in Canada. In reviewing the *Yearbook of the Arts in Canada in 1936* for *New Frontier* (Feb. 1937), Kennedy gave his summary of Canadian life:

More than one tenth of our population is subsisting on direct relief, subject to malnutrition and indignity, preyed on by insecurity, salting their slender ration with despair. Hundreds of thousands in the western drought areas are people without hope. We have had a Hunger March that will be history when much of the delicate personal writing in this book is forgotten. Strife, unrest and brutal persecution of minorities and whole communities in company towns are rife. Fascism is afoot in Quebec. Our middle class is living on the crumbling edge of security, its livelihood threatened, its precious freedom of thought and speech being rapidly curtailed. The virtue of its white collar no longer stands between it and the plight of the laboring class.

Yet when Kennedy attempted to deal with a Canadian politician in a poem, he filled it with propagandist clichés, talking of "cossacks," "Bosses," "Industry's Captains." His best lines in "Epitaph For A Canadian Statesman," (*New Frontier*, April, 1936) were addressed to the apologists for Mr. Bennett; the method of juxtaposition emphasized the (to the poet) ludicrous figure presented by his political presence:

> Draft plaintive eulogies for him
> Whose swallow tails and penguin paunch
> Are fluttering with the cherubim.

Much of Kennedy's political poetry was imperative in tone. To read it is to subject oneself to exhortations and commands but these offer nothing more than vague general revolutionary directions. A poem with the title "Summons For This Generation" (*New Frontier*, April, 1936) one might expect to be an hortatory and ringing exultation of revolutionary fervour but in fact the language in the poem is little removed from that of *The Shrouding*:

> Revoke your ebb's dispersal with arrayed
> Bright flesh on stalwart scaffolding of chalk,
> With hair grown subtly to a thatch, the scooped
> Low-buttressed skull that roofs the wits the walk
> Of the time-ghost, with vigorous grouped
> Limbs, with wrists, with hands alertly splayed.

Yet in another poem, "Memorial To The Defending" (*New Frontier*, February, 1937), the image of the body is used more satisfactorily in terms of a barricade and sustains the notion that the single human is the factor which will be the real revolutionary force:

> You Comrades rearing separate barricades
> Of bone that's prompt to splinter, blood to spurt
> And intricate, swift nerves that shock and dull
> At blast of thermite and the bullet's rip.

The trouble facing a political poet, despite his insistence on description of actual revolutionary fighting, the corruption and tyranny of the ruling class and the apathy of the majority, is to refrain from being purely negative; he must offer some solution, avoiding the pitfalls of propaganda and the clichés of Marxist dogma. Kennedy tends to fall back on the idyllic vision of a left-wing Utopia in optimistic generalizations, as he does in this poem:

> This love will yet set garlands round your names;
> This sacrifice bear increment of joy
> When the clean world you die for casts it [sic] slough.

This is a pitfall that Auden's political verse also falls into: his poem "Spain" contains idyllic pictures of the workers taking over "tomorrow" as opposed to "today the struggle." Kennedy was quick to see the effect of this in Auden's poem when he reviewed it: "It is remote studio stuff that might just as well have been written in bedroom slippers at home" (*New Frontier*, September, 1937). The same comment could well apply to some of Kennedy's attempts at political verse. He saw the dangers of trying to build a political poem by means of an intellectual system of symbols and images, as he stated in the same review:

It would be a better work if free of the formal emotional restraint, and engagement with intellectual symbols that are very fine in their place but which make for a static response in the trained poetry reader, and utter bewilderment in the untrained.

Certainly there is little emotional restraint in Kennedy's political poetry but too often this lack leads him into sentimentality or hysteria, as in the prose poem, "Revolutionary Greeting" (*New Frontier*, November, 1936) which deals with various abstract qualities (beauty, strength, eagerness, comfort, courage) possessed by individual comrades; each stanza describes an idealized Comrade in romantic terms ending with one summarizing abstraction, "the workers of the world have need of beauty," until the final stanza repeats the slogan: "be fearless, hurling the slogans, scornful of violence, urging mass action, raising the banner: WORKERS OF THE WORLD UNITE! The workers of the world have need of courage." This evokes static response because the romantic diction, at times cliché-ridden, descends to this propagandist call and does not elevate the reader to an acceptance of the rightness of the appeal.

Kennedy understood the difficulties without ever fully conquering them. He insists in "Advice To A Young Poet" (*New Frontier*, March, 1937) that a poet must fix his attention on "immediates":

> Cling eagerly to grass,
>   Fix passion on stone,
> Hook living hands on air,
>   Thrust tentacles on loam,

> And bind your breastbone fast
> To men you never knew:

but the language of the poem degenerates into slogan-like phrases, even though the poem picks up the opening image at the end:

> nameless men whose blood
> Nourished the trampled plant
> Set precedent to reach
> Whether we die or not.

We have seen that he was most successful in his political writing when he used a method of juxtaposition together with a simple pattern of images derived basically from his early volume, *The Shrouding*, as in "New Comrade," and in two other poems, "You, Spanish Comrade" (*New Frontier*, November, 1936) and "Calling Eagles" (*New Frontier*, June, 1937). Both use the image of the eagle as revolutionary, enabling the poet to draw on a reference to attacks from the air and also to the whole world of nature. The first poem opens with a fine image of an eagle's attack, placing the reader in the revolutionary situation and even managing to use the somewhat vague term "freedom" with telling effect:

> Swing, eagle, high over barricades and plunge
> boldly, talon and beak flash golden
> in Toledo sunlight, bayonet and beak
> fierce thrust at fascist throats, the rifle butts
> wing-buffeting, whirling, splintering for freedom.

He doesn't quite avoid descending into hackneyed phrasing in the rest of the stanza but by the end of the second stanza he can revert to a positive use of *Shrouding* imagery in depicting the optimism of ultimate victory in lines romantic and verging on the sentimental without finally dropping into sentimentality:

> you build foundations here with bone for granite,
> spilled blood and flesh for mortar, and the bright
> mouths of dead girls to keep a memory green:

Thus prepared, the reader, I think, will accept the close of the poem with its vision of idyllic peasant life (given this particular Spanish situation without applying it as a general Utopian solution to the world's problems) :

> a place there'll be for work and skill and learning,
> for peasants turning earth no locust bares,
> and girls with flowers new children springing tall.

In "Calling Eagles," a statement against isolationism and intellectual ivory-towerism, eagles are symbolic of intellectuals:

> Slanting the ragged peaks of the mind, Eagles,
> Swift thinkers, readers in books and the bones of
>   nature, construing
> Life at its conflux, observing nebula, sifting fact from
>   suppose, swooping
> With noble talons arched for the scrap of truth.

This intellectual energy should be converted to the cause of humanity in the fight against political treachery "where Spain tangles in blood," "And fascist madmen rattle gaoler's keys." This middle section of the poem with its catalogue of political miseries is enough to save the poem from collapsing under a welter of vague and romantic abstractions (and even a hint of condescension in the use of the word "groundlings," even though it is to be taken in opposition to the heights attained by the eagle):

> Drop from your eyrie, spurning the misted heights,
> Plunge to the valley where life is and verdure,
> Join with the groundlings, multitudes, with hope and
>   passion
> Lifting their fists with the steel clenched, towering
> A new state from the crumble and wrack of the old.

Kennedy tries to emphasize that this struggle will be an intellectual as well as a physical fight. Intellectual strength is needed, not sheer brute force, to overthrow the old system:

> There is work for your strong beaks and the thundering
>   wings,
> For the clean flight of the mind and the sharp
>   perception:

> *There is only a glacial death on the lonely crags.*

Miriam Waddington selected this poem as an example of protest poetry of the thirties which was poor in comparison with much of A. M. Klein's work at that time. "Kennedy's intentions may have been good, but his poem is sentimental and false."[1] The poem may indeed topple over into sentimentality at times but because of its insistence on detail at the centre, it does not become a "false" poem.

---

[1]"The Cloudless Day: The Radical Poems of A. M. Klein," *Tamarack Review*, Autumn, 1967, 85.

3. F. R. Scott

THE POET IN QUEBEC TODAY

F. R. SCOTT

My early poetry was very influenced by the geography of Quebec. Coming back from Oxford, where for the first time in my life I was brought into direct contact with the European tradition, in which one soaked up the human achievements of great individuals and great nations past and present, and where always one was drawn back toward antiquity, I found Quebec presented a totally different kind of challenge. Here nothing great seemed to have been achieved in human terms. I was shocked by the ugliness of the cities and buildings by comparison with those that I had recently lived in, and there seemed so little that one wished to praise or draw inspiration from in our social environment or past history. But the Laurentian country was wonderful, open, empty, vast, and speaking a kind of eternal language in its mountains, rivers and lakes. I knew that these were the oldest mountains in the world, and that their rounded valleys and peaks were the result of long submersion under continents of ice. Geologic time made ancient civilizations seem but yesterday's picnic. This caught my imagination and I tried to express some of this feeling in what I call my Laurentian poems. It was a form of "internalization of the wilderness," and it sufficed me at first for poetic inspiration.

As I became more involved in the human society about me, particularly after the great financial crash of 1929, the

ensuing depression and the emergence of revolutionary
and reform political movements in which I participated,
I found that I reacted negatively in my writing and turned
easily to satire. The satire was the holding up of the
existing society against standards one was formulating in
one's mind for a more perfect society. It was not revolu-
tionary poetry; it was satiric poetry, which is quite a dif-
ferent thing, though somewhat allied.

A LETTER FROM F. R. SCOTT TO
ANNE HEBERT

Robert Frost has said that the poetry is what is lost in
translation. This is a truth but, I believe—and your letter
encourages me in the belief—not the whole truth. Not all
is lost or need be lost. Translation is itself an art, and one
which surely has helped every writer to understand much
of the other literatures of the world. Perhaps today we
need to practise and encourage this art more than ever,
since otherwise we deprive ourselves not only of great
experiences but of that mutual respect between races
which is an imperative in the modern world. In Canada
we have particular need of it, depending as we do so much
upon the two chief cultural traditions which are at the
base of our native arts. For the prose writer the problem
is relatively simple, and the English Canadian can now
enjoy a growing body of literature written in French
Canada and presented in his own language. Bilingualism
being more widespread among French Canadians, the
reverse translation is not so essential, though this too is
coming. But the poet speaks a language which even his

From *Tamarack Review* (Summer 1962), 73-4. Copyright 1962 by
Tamarack Review. Reprinted by permission of *Tamarack Review* and
the author.

own compatriots are often unable to understand. To translate him is the greatest challenge the translator can face.

Your remarks upon the art of translation were to me especially illuminating, and hold up an ideal which I think every translator should always keep before him. I believe with you that he must first appreciate the original poem, must feel it deeply inside himself as the author feels it in the process of creating it. The translation then becomes another making, demanding the same kind of ability and vision as the author possessed, with the same careful selection of words, phrases and sounds. The difference is that the translator is given an external criterion of the appropriateness of his writing, in the poem to be translated. He writes, as it were, to order, yet must create while obeying the order. He is unfree and yet free at the same time. My good fortune is not only to have such a poem beside me as my guide, but yourself too to sharpen my perception when I fail to see what you saw and to feel as you felt. The "dialogue between author and translator," as you point out, can thus be carried on between us directly, and little by little what is in your poem can be made to express itself more and more in my language. At the end, however, there will still be something unsaid by me. This is where your poem is left standing alone.

REVIEW OF *OVERTURE*

E. K. BROWN

Those of us who have watched for the appearance of Mr. F. R. Scott's poems in the magazines and anthologies of the past two decades have also looked forward to the year

From "Letters in Canada: 1945—Poetry" by E. K. Brown. From *University of Toronto Quarterly*, XV (April 1946), 269-272. Copyright 1946 by the University of Toronto Press. Reprinted by permission of the University of Toronto Press and the estate of the author.

which would bring a collection of them. That it would be an impressive book no one could have doubted. It is more impressive than I had expected—it reveals that Mr. Scott is among the few modern poets who can be read at length with unwearied technical pleasure, with intellectual satisfaction, and with unresting poetical excitement. *Overture* is one of the best volumes of poetry this country has seen, and what I have elsewhere described as the wall that Americans have raised against Canadian poetry should not prove high enough to keep out Mr. Scott. His poetry is the expression of a man who is living intensely and sensitively on all levels, spiritual, intellectual, political and sensual. It is the expression of a man who, very much a citizen of his own country, is also a citizen of the world. I do not know of any book in prose or verse in the past five years which more powerfully shows that we in Canada, or some of us, enough of us to matter, have come of age.

The first great strength of this poetry is a core of belief. No one who knows the history of poetry can doubt that it is of immense advantage to a poet that he should believe firmly, and that his belief should be comprehensive, enlarging to the spirit, and so substantial as to command at the very least the reader's ungrudged respect. It is, above all, of use to the poet that he should believe in mind, not the *siccum lumen* (as I need scarely say) but mind as Wordsworth or Coleridge conceived it. "Every time," wrote A. C. Bradley forty years ago in *English Poetry and German Philosophy in the Age of Wordsworth*, "has the defects of its qualities; but those periods in which, and those men in whom, the mind is strongly felt to be great, see more and see deeper than others. . . . And when the greatness of the mind is strongly felt, it is great and works wonders." The belief in the greatness of the mind has been rare in recent poetry, Canadian or other. It is strong in Mr. Scott's.

It rings out again and again. "To Certain Friends" is addressed to men with comfortably full minds but no

intention or ability to do anything with them. It begins
with agreeable lightness on the surface:

> They show great zeal collecting the news and statistics.
> They know far more about every question than I do,
> But their knowledge of how to use knowledge grows
>   smaller and smaller.

> They make a virtue of having an open mind,
> Open to endless arrivals of other men's suggestions,
> To the rain of facts that deepens the drought of the will.

> Above all they fear the positive formation of opinion,
> The essential choice that acts as a mental compass,
> The clear perception of the road to the receding horizon.

Mr. Scott has not been unobservant when he has attended
the meetings of our learned societies, or listened to the
patter of comment in our senior common-rooms. At the
close of the poem the note is a deeper one and angry:

> They will grow old searching to avoid conclusions,
> Refusing to learn by living, to test by trying,
> Letting opportunities slip from their tentative fingers.

> Till one day, after the world has tired of waiting,
> While they are busy arguing about the obvious,
> A half-witted demagogue will walk away with their
>   children.

This poem is such an attack on a disease of the mind as
only a man who passionately believes in its right use could
conceive.

The mind, Mr. Scott holds, will help us to plan and
establish a great society. To do so we must drop much that
has charm, for the charm, he thinks, is a tie with things
which are far from charming, antiquated, crippling to the
mind, intolerable to the alert moral sense. I continue to
think that Mr. Scott is for dropping too much. In the title-
poem he is for dropping Mozart, by which he means the
states of being that Mozart can arouse in those who love
his work. He is for dropping tea-parties and bric-a-brac—

partly this is mere sentiment, for Mr. Scott like the other
poets of his group has ears that are closed to the beauty
of Victorian poetry, and eyes resentfully critical of the
Victorian minor arts. Perhaps the examples of both had an
almost peculiar badness in Montreal and Quebec when
Mr. Scott was growing up. But the mind he will never
drop:

> And if the ultimate I, the inner mind,
> The only shelter proof against attack
> Sustain these days, carry this banner out
> To the clumsy dawn: a green seed
> Lies on the ground under a leafless tree.

Many of the poems express Mr. Scott's socialist plan for
the great society. They escape the flatness which curses so
much proletarian verse, partly because Mr. Scott generally
avoids abstract polysyllables, rhetorical exclamations, and
all the rest of the dreary apparatus of inflated prose which
some versifiers demand that we accept as being a finer
distillation of poetry than Yeats's lyricism. The essence of
Mr. Scott's social ideal is mind in society, the planned
society; and in his way of conceiving this he is no naive
rationalist, he is indeed very much of a mystic. For partisan
reasons he would not perhaps appreciate the comparison;
but his "socialism" is much akin to the Prime Minister's,
one of whose recurrent quotations is: "We are members
one of another." By both political leaders mind is con-
ceived in a generous sense, inhibiting neither to poetry nor
to religion.

There is one reflective lyric in the collection which I
should set beside Mr. Leo Kennedy's "Words for a Resur-
rection" and Mr. Pratt's "Silences," that is, in the very
highest range of reflective lyrical verse in the past quarter-
century. This is "Advice":

> Beware the casual need
> By which the heart is bound;
> Pluck out the quickening seed
> That falls on stony ground.

Forgo the shallow gain,
The favour of an hour,
Escape, by early pain,
The death before the flower.

There is no reason why this, in its almost perfect purity,
should ever age; and its wisdom will stand the strictest test,
and emerge a living thing. There are a number of poems
in this vein, some of them weakened by the closing lines
in which Mr. Scott almost always tries for a climax and
sometimes comes to ruin, others almost as perfect as
"Advice." Among the triumphs I should place "Dedica-
tion," "November Pool" and "Below Quebec." Among the
poems with disappointing endings are "Calvary," "Devoir
Molluscule" and "Union." In "Union" the three final
lines seem an obvious appendage, and I suggest to Mr.
Scott that he considers the poem as it stands and then the
poem shorn of its appendage; perhaps he will agree that
everything he wished to convey is conveyed without it, and
that by dropping it he will enable the poem to rest in
perfect proportion. "Teleological" is, I think, a poem of
an inferior texture throughout; but in it also the final
lines are lost.

F. R. SCOTT AND THE MODERN POETS

LOUIS DUDEK

The first quality which will strike the reader in the poetry
of F. R. Scott is a clear-sightedness which is both winning
in its directness and limited in its scope. The reader will
not be surprised. It is a quality which in one form or

"F. R. Scott and the Modern Poets" by Louis Dudek. From *Northern Review*, IV (Dec.-Jan. 1950-51), 4-15. Reprinted by permission of the author, who has made some stylistic revisions in the article for this collection.

another has always been characteristic of Canadian poetry. Hardly a sign of "native vigour," it may go well with certain beauties which symbolize it—the transparent icicle, the cold snow, the autumn air. We exploit our innocence to make it a virtue. Adjudged critically (with no special application to Frank Scott) as a lack of complication in feeling and thinking, a willingness to be satisfied with surfaces and single facets of things, it may be a clue to our greatest needs. We suffer the simplifications in a partly isolated culture of patterns and tendencies which exist in a more complicated form outside: single currents of what is or was happening in the literatures of England, France, America. John Sutherland has suggested recently that we could deal with Canadian writers by comparing them with prototypes whom they resemble in the parent literatures; ironically, this might give us an insight not only into the individual quality of our Canadian writing but also at times into English and American poetry. Canada might provide an experimental field in which trends of British and American poetry find a clear and interesting form of expression. The poetry of F. R. Scott offers a favourable test case; and on this theory I will try to draw a parallel between his poetry and some of the tendencies in English poetry in our time.

Scott's poetry, as it has appeared since 1926, in the *McGill Fortnightly Review,* in the *Canadian Forum,* in our literary magazines, and in the book *Overture* (1945), is an example in our literature of the turning away of one generation from another, in this case the son departing from the ways of the father. Scott's father, Frederick George Scott, was a noted Archdeacon of the Anglican church, a Canadian padre at the front in World War I, a highly-regarded poet in his own right. He belonged to the same generation and literary period as Archibald Lampman and Bliss Carman, whose successors trail in a long line to the Canadian Authors' Association membership today. A poet of integrity, imaginative vigour and respectable versification, Frederick George Scott, who died in 1944, represents for the Canada of 1890-1920 the solid Victorian tradition of faith, earnestness and moral energy we admire in Carlyle, Ruskin and Tennyson, but which by the nineties was being shaken by the first generation of rebels, the aesthetes of the *Yellow Book*, and after 1910 was further undermined, if not totally demolished, by the so-called "moderns" of various schools. It is to his father as a representative of Victorian earnestness and faith that F. R. Scott, on the satirical side of his poetry, stands in striking antithesis; and therefore his position in Canadian poetry, curious as it may seem, corresponds in effect to the combined Eliot and Auden generation in England. To put it simply, he is our first representative modern poet.

The outburst of modern poetry in England can be seen clearly from one point of view if it is understood as a revolt against that class which had set the pace in all things human from the French Revolution, the class which had replaced the aristocracy. We are now at a point when we are beginning to regret the loss of the upper bourgeoisie, and when the true content of our literature—the effort to save a civilizing tradition—finds itself helpless without the real support of a social class which might embody it; but modern literature arose in the spirit of a lively rebellion, the rebellion of bourgeois and middle class artists against the worn-out literary and social accoutrements of the respectable middle class. Bourgeois culture was first undermined by members of its own class (as the eighteenth century aristocracy had been), and today its ghost is being nostalgically revived in the prospect of a grim demagogic future: the civilization which the bourgeoisie has carried thus far needs to find new hands to bear it forward against the threatening barbarism, either of capitalistic advertising-democracy or police-state communism. T. S. Eliot, most prominently, has taken a stand in defence of a class society based on permanently established élites, although he is aware that the bourgeoisie, or upper middle class, has passed, or "is commonly said to be passing."

Whether it is "past, or passing, or to come," I have heard a friend, a minor German poet of the last generation, repeat sadly that European culture of the time before 1910 was an Age of Gold which has been lost to us forever; and Stephen Spender, in a lecture, recently reflected that we have lost in the bourgeoisie both a support and a valid citadel of attack, so that without it modern poetry is the unbounded homeless thing it is. As I write, an article has come out in *Partisan Review* (December, 1950) laying on the door of the "intellectuals" some of the blame for the political consequences which have followed the collapse of the bourgeoisie. Hannah Arendt writes in "The Mob and the Elite": ". . . only an inherent fundamental shortcoming of character in the intellectual, '*la trahison des clercs*' (J. Benda), or a perverse self-hatred of the spirit, accounted for the delight with which this élite accepted the 'ideas' of the mob."

But this is 1950. We must turn back for sharp contrast to D. H. Lawrence's "How Beastly the Bourgeois is"; T. S. Eliot's "Prufrock," "Aunt Helen," "Cousin Nancy," satires of that bourgeoisie whose ghost we would now exorcise; Pound's "Portrait d'une femme," and the satires in "Hugh Selwyn Mauberley" and "Moeurs contemporaines"; or any of a score of poems in the Auden and Spender decade.

> Where is the bourgeois, the backbone of our race?
> Bent double with lackeying, the joints out of place;
> Behind bluffs and lucky charms hiding to evade
> An overdue audit, anaemic, afraid. . . .
> They're paying for death on the instalment plan
> Who hoped to go higher and failed to be men.
>
> *C. Day Lewis*

We can put it this way: the bourgeoisie in its last stages, with its amenities, its pieties, its Sunday morning gravity, proliferated and perpetuated a nauseating, decayed poetry of mediocre moralizing, philosophizing and lyricizing—the last dregs of romanticism—against which the moderns raised their war, a war "against all sorts of mortmain" (Pound); and therefore their iconoclasm in poetry implied a social break with the bourgeoisie—a break whose consequences are now being regretted. And as we know, it was by resort to satire and to wholesale caricature, as always when a historical rejection takes place, that this war was fought.

In Canada, this war against the effete bourgeois tradition is not yet finished. But its pattern here is the same; so that by contrasting the work of F. R. Scott with that of his father the relationship of one generation to the other becomes clear.

The method of F. R. Scott, the modernist, is satire. Where his senior had sung vigorously of the life of respectability and its wholesome virtues, he himself throws out persistent jibes at the career bourgeois who makes a success of playing the politics of the ruling class and ends with LL.D.'s and finally a British peerage. In "Boston Tea Party: 1940" he takes a whack at Eliot's own Bostonians:

> While D.A.R.'s and Ph.D.'s
> And "How-d'ye-do's" and "Is-that so's"
> Are wafted on a scented breeze
> That piles the orchid on the rose.

Where his father had been moved to the old Wordsworthian pantheistic theme,

> Something in my inmost thinking
>   Tells me I am one with you,
> For a subtle bond is linking
>   Nature's offspring through and through . . .

F. R. Scott, in one of his poems,

> Brings a reminder from the barren north
> Of the eternal lifeless processes.

Where his father's poetry was deeply and earnestly moved
by an explicit religious faith, so that he could say after
reading Darwin's *Origin of Species,*

> The pulse of our life is in tune with the rhythm
>   of forces that beat
> In the surf of the furthest star's sea and are spent
>   and regathered to spend,

F. R. Scott presents the coming of life in satirical terms:

> Note, please, the embryo.
>   Unseeing
> It survives into being.
> *Elan vital,*
> Thyroid, gonads, *et al.,*
> preserve the unities. . . .

And where Frederick George Scott could sing,

> O England of our Fathers and England of our sons . . .
> For Empire has been ours of old and Empire ours
>   shall be. . . .

the prophecy was not fulfilled in the sons, for F. R. Scott
waxes satirical about our subjected colonialism of mind
and throws overboard the virtues of

> Obedience, Loyalty, and Love of Kings.

And finally, where his father had been reconciled to the
political and economic status quo, F. R. Scott is an ardent
socialist, and the primary aim of his satirical poetry is to
spur on the people of Canada to political action and to
a radical solution of their problems—problems whose solu-
tion in his opinion is indefinitely postponed by the cor-
porate capitalist bourgeoisie of Canada.

Now, there is a vast difference in character between the
satirical poetry of F. R. Scott and the comic-satirical poetry
of Pound or Eliot or even the satire of the Auden-
MacNeice generation, which it more closely resembles.
The social satire of Pound and Eliot presents an exas-

perated digression, which is not really a digression, from
the conventional subjects of poetry into a social miasma
which lay at the root of their literary troubles. In the case
of Pound, through what appears as a digression we arrive
at a conception of the organic unity between society in all
its ramifications (especially economics) and the fine arts.
In the case of Eliot, social analysis leads him to a religious
point of view which becomes the subject of great poetry.
Perhaps it is only through this sort of "digression"—refus-
ing to lose the artistic purpose—that the political subject
can become successful in poetry, as in Dante, Milton,
Wordsworth. Now, in the poems of F. R. Scott politics
assumes the central declarative position for the poet: he
becomes too obviously a socialist writing socialistic verse,
a man with a political purpose, not primarily a poet dis-
tracted by the times into shouting out a political message.
Of course, something of the same narrowing of objectives
is to be found in the English poets of the thirties; and yet
a re-reading of their work—or a glance at C. Day Lewis'
A Hope for Poetry—will show how much more severe is
the self-limitation of the Canadian poet. Here, then, is the
one-sidedness and simplification of the Canadian position.

Moreover, the comic-satirical poetry coming out of
England quivers with a decadent, now-uncoordinated life
interwoven with literary tradition, a complex class-struc-
tured society, an age-old institutionalized religion: the
social satire of Eliot and of the Auden generation, is a
plant with a thick and tangled mess of roots hanging from
it. That of our Canadian poet, true to Canadian life, is
much more simple and unilateral. It is like the clear air,
the wide open spaces, the unclouded mind of many
Canadians. Some of his verse is a pleasant sort of socialistic
vers de société, brilliant in its cleverness, but one feels that
on the literal, unimaginative and un-literary plane which
Scott has chosen, not much can be done. The verse derives
in form ultimately from the T. S. Eliot poems of the
Sweeney period (1918) and Pound of the quatrains in

"Mauberley" and "Moeurs Contemporaines" (going back to Gauthier's *Emaux et Camées*); but it lacks the implications that make these poems of Eliot and Pound sometimes the most difficult of all that they have written. In some of the poems Scott has also adopted the conversational style of Auden and the poets of the thirties; but we now begin to see that there was little gain to poetry in the prosaic chit-chat of Auden and his friends—their best work is of the tighter and more introspective kind. So here again the defect is aggravated and simplified; the blank explicit directness of Scott's satirical verse limits it to a period in time, and the crisp meters bring to mind a clever preacher of the Enlightenment talking down in couplets to his dull brethren. The whole situation is analogical.

Yet in spite of all this, I think that the best of Scott's satirical poems—such poems as "Mural," "Tourist Time," "Lest we Forget," and "The Canadian Authors Meet"— are poems which will be read amongst us for a long time. These verses sparkle with a sharp wit which might best be described in the same terms that Scott uses to describe a Mozart sonata:

> The bright
> Clear notes fly like sparks through the air
> And trace a flickering pattern of music there.

They are excellent poems in their kind. However, it is not for his satirical verse that Scott deserves the most serious attention as a poet. His best work is in the serious lyrics in the book *Overture*. It is this we must now consider.

The English poets, after the release provided by satire turned back to what we might conventionally describe as "positions previously prepared": Eliot to Anglicanism, Pound to a dedication to the arts in a framework of history, in *The Cantos* (an epic poem to show when the arts and civilization are sound, when corrupt). The Auden and Spender generation has followed the same general course as Pound and Eliot. Not that the positions to which these poets retreated were simply old and established positions: the "retreat" could just as validly be called an advance. No one ever goes back into the past; we can only *use* something in the past to carry us forward. The Anglicanism of Eliot is a revival resulting from a contemporary sense of necessity, a desire to shore up a dying culture, and to find salvation beyond this Wasteland and death; and the aestheticism of Pound is certainly unlike that of the followers of Pater, it is involved with a historical and realistic criticism of society, a demand for total health in life and art. And yet at the same time the relation of both poets to the past is very clear, the first to Newman and Matthew Arnold, the second to "art for art." They now represent the counter-revolution, establishing gains and salvaging the past.

We find a similar sort of retreat to positions previously prepared in the poetry of F. R. Scott written in a personal and serious vein. Not that this stage of his writing follows in point of time the satirical poems, nor that Scott ever abandons the satirical stage of his writing to turn to a high-serious poetry—perhaps the absence of such a forthright about-face is in itself characteristic of the Canadian weakening of the intensity of the modern tensions; but when he writes his lyrics we hear another man speaking, not the social reformer, but a muted poet of personal experience and of the place of this experience in the frame of human destiny. In these poems, and they deserve the most careful analytic reading, Scott returns to the situation and subject matter of the poetry of an older generation, really the generation of his father, but making the modifications in tone and outlook which establish these poems as entirely of our own time.

Like the affirmations of the English poets, moreover, this return is not simply a return to the bourgeois tradition

of the forefathers. It is an affirmation and a search that
in the English poets can be as much related to Pascal and
to Dante as to Cardinal Newman; to twelfth century
troubadors as to Swinburne; to Renaissance humanism as
to nineteenth century rationalism and the problems of
faith. The bulwarks of defence stand before an older and
richer civilization than that of the bourgeoisie—although
that class has been its most recent support. In F. R. Scott,
the past and the needs of the present are similarly united.

As a single illustration, here are a few verses from a
now-forgotten poem of the late Archdeacon Scott:

> Only the mountains rear their forms,
>   Silent and grim and bold;
> To them the voices of the storms
>   Are as a tale re-told.
>
> They saw the stars in heaven hung,
>   They heard the great Sea's birth,
> They know the ancient pain that wrung
>   The entrails of the earth.
>
> Sprung from great Nature's royal lines,
>   They share her deep repose—
> Their rugged shoulders robed in pines,
>   Their foreheads crowned with snows.

The Laurentian Shield is here a symbol of the ageless
earth; the poem, swinging in Tennysonian fashion be-
tween scientific wonder (albeit without anxiety) and
implicit faith, plays on a theme which is recurrent in the
poetry of the elder Scott: the imaginative contemplation
of geological time and man's career in time and space.
Now let us turn to a companion passage in the poetry of
F. R. Scott:

> far voices
> and fretting leaves
> this music the
> hillside gives

but in the deep
Laurentian river
an elemental song
for ever

a quiet calling
of no mind
out of long aeons
when dust was blind
and ice hid sound

only a moving
with no note
granite lips
a stone throat

Here is the same symbol and the same idea of earth history
—the history of that ancient Canadian earth and its frozen
north—but used in the context of a contemporary sense
of loss, of groping, of refusal to accept anything but the
stark realities of scientific truth. Though the security of
faith is gone, the poet has returned to the same place to
contemplate the same problem. Now there is no answer.

This searching in the old grounds of belief runs through
F. R. Scott's poetry:

Fearfully the mind's hands dig
In the debris of thought, for the lovely body of faith.

It is especially remarkable in the poems using a Christian
symbolism. At times, he almost believes that "truth stands
naked" again; or in an airliner rides where "Man, the
lofty worm, tunnels his latest clay"; but the final and last-
ing statement is that of the "eternal lifeless processes" in
one of his finest poems:

Come, flaunt the brief prerogative of life
Dip your small civilized foot in this cold water
And ripple, for a moment, the smooth surface of time.

However, one cannot help feeling as one reads this
poetry that it is not all of Scott that went into the writing

of these poems; or at any rate that too much of his energy
had been drained in another direction. It is as if Canada
were not yet ready to allow a first-rate mind to devote
itself wholly to poetry. In F. R. Scott, the moral energy,
the active part of the "faith" which he had inherited, was
turned to the work of social analysis and political recon-
struction. As a leader in the CCF Party he attempted to
write the poem of political reality which Edmund Wilson
once predicted would someday replace poetry entirely;
and this could only be done at the expense of the poem
of imagination on the printed page.

This choice between the political and the artistic pros-
pect is stated most explicitly in the poem "Overture,"
which appeared in the book *New Provinces* (1936) and
which gives the title to F. R. Scott's first published book:

> But how shall I hear old music? This is an hour
> Of new beginnings, concepts warring for power,
> Decay of systems—the tissue of art is torn
> With overtures of an era being born.
>
> And this perfection which is less yourself
> Than Mozart, seems a trinket on a shelf,
> A pretty octave played before a window
> Beyond whose curtain grows a world crescendo.

Who does not remember the days when this was the thing
to say? The narrowing down of objectives, the "social con-
sciousness" that pushed everything aside before its historic
"necessity," these seemed inevitable for the poet in the
1930s; but in Canada, a country with a minor literature
just in its beginning, such an idea imported from abroad
was bound to be the more constricting and incomplete.

There is a tiny poem by F. R. Scott entitled "Book-
worm" which ironically comments on the literary-minded
lover saying goodnight, a parody aimed at T. S. Eliot:

> Let us cast over this natural event
> The drapery of a literary allusion.

And yet, consider how studded with literary allusions is the poetry of Eliot, Pound, Auden! And what is the "natural event," reality, without imagination and the colourings of time? In this epigram we have the dilemma of the modern poet, caught in the split between imagination and reality, which runs across the *Wasteland* and other poems of T. S. Eliot. In F. R. Scott, the "natural event" embraces all the optimistic action and policy leading toward a political future, stated in realistic satirical verse; and what is left to the serious poetry is a wish for completeness that is never satisfied. The two are never made to burn together as in T. S. Eliot's poetry. But the total imaginable reality, which is so much more than any "natural event," is precisely what the poet desires.

The feeling of being "cut off from wholeness," stated in the poem "Windfall," and the desire to recapture according to the romantic formula

> Whispers of a greener life
> When the heart burned

touches painfully on this subject. It is beautifully expressed, both directly and indirectly, in poems such as "Full Valleys," "Autumnal," "Bedside," "Lost Syllable," "Grey Morning," "Old Song," "Surfaces." One should read these over and over at the cost of omitting a good line or two in the pages of Scott's satirical verse. They express the search that is in all the best poems of our time.

The tone of these poems will be readily compared with that prevailing in T. S. Eliot, but this is not because anything is borrowed: it is the emotional situation, the kind of spiritual martyrdom which is the same. T. S. Eliot makes great poetical capital out of it, or in spite of it, largely by his wealth of "literary allusion." He relates his dilemma in the wasteland of the modern world to images of a magnificent past. In F. R. Scott's poetry, however, the wasteland remains one of barren rock and cold time.

The result is a frozen poem that may be described as the lyric fossilized, a poem fashioned concisely as a lyric, but which is not an expressed emotion, hence a contradiction in terms. The quiet despair of some of Hardy's late lyrics, and some of Edwin Arlington Robinson's, are of this kind. They give us the lyric pared to the bone, the remnant of emotion, an evidence of checkmated vitality, of the frustration of something vital in modern living.

Successful emotion—not the cerebral and baffled pain which most of us know as "feeling"—is in love with objects in the world, throws bits of reality on the page; it is imaginative; that is, it attaches itself to the images of objects. It reasons with shapes, sounds, and actions. Bourgeois culture was languishing in an emotionless and decently smothered poetry of cosmic abstractions and abstract Christian virtues, at best of nature references which were unexperienced and unvisualized. Then came Imagism, Chinese poetry (as analyzed in a famous forgotten essay by Fenollosa), and finally even modern psychology, to tell us that this was death, not life. The real image is the live thing. And so there is a constant and courageous effort in the lyrics of F. R. Scott to achieve the precise image, to concretize the emotion of the poem: for example, "North Stream" may very well be compared with the pure imagery of a poem by William Carlos Williams. But the total effect of Scott's lyrics is that of precision and of intelligence of a high order, not of poetic richness. In terms of William Blake's geography of the soul, one might say that, in literary performance, the intellect, or reason, had encroached too far on the realms of the senses, the imagination, and the active emotions. Or in Shelley's language, poetry had not found the

> . . . strength to pierce the guarded wit,
> And pass into the panting heart beneath.

But this is a general criticism that we can make of a good deal of twentieth-century poetry. At least we have the fuller objective in our mind.

And sometimes in Scott's poetry there almost comes an intensification to that white heat which is wholeness, "the whole skylight of thought . . . the boundless uplands of art"; but it is momentary. It brings to mind the assured and self-confident energy of imagination and moral will which was in some of the poetry of Frederick George Scott, his father. We have it in the recent excellent poem "Lakeshore" which was printed in *Northern Review*:

> Sometimes, upon a crowded street
> I feel the endless rain come down,
> And in the old magnetic sound
> I heard the opening of a gate
> That loosens all the seven seas. . . .

And we have it, too, in the closing lines of the poem "Spring, 1941" included in the book *Overture*:

> Drop token loads, but save the harder man,
> Eyes to stare at the sun, heart's leap and love.

. . . .

> Are we born too? . . . Can we be born
> Like sun from night, a fructifying fire?
> Turn dark to fecundation, there is power!
> And roll, roll over the springing world.

I believe that in this, and poems like it, there is a hope for Canadian poetry which we shall see more and more realized in the years to come.

REVIEW OF *SIGNATURE*

MILTON WILSON

I've been trying to find the appropriate adjective for F. R. Scott's poetry. What has sent me on the hunt is his fourth and latest collection, *Signature*. Certainly there are a good many Canadian poets more "sensitive," "imaginative," "original," "enterprising," "complex," "brilliant"—both from his own generation (he is 65) and generations since. The process of elimination of adjectives could go on for some time. But I can think of an important word or two that might stay put, though they aren't exactly new. He is our most "civilized" poet, even (in one sense of the word) our most "classical." He is a cultivated, humane member of society who (among other things) happens to write poetry. His poems are illuminations on the margins of a life, and they exist for its sake and not vice versa. But there is nothing of the slap-dash amateur about Scott. He is a workman responsible to his materials and tools and concerned to make the best of them within the given conditions. These are mostly occasional poems, if you will: under no illusions about their limitations, but usually managing to deliver a good deal more than they assume.

> I looked the sun straight in the eye.
> He put on dark glasses.

Perhaps the right bland, all-purpose adjective would be "readable," by which I mean that he's one of the few poets that I could sit down and read at any time and at any place. *Signature* is a heterogeneous collection, like *Overture* (1945) and *Events and Signals* (1954), but less distinguished than the latter I would say. I wish it included

From "Letters in Canada: 1964—Poetry" by Milton Wilson. From *University of Toronto Quarterly*, XXXIV (July 1965), 358-9. Copyright 1965 by the University of Toronto Press. Reprinted by permission of the author and the University of Toronto Press.

more comic pieces, but I guess Scott hasn't had time to
restock since he exhausted his supply in *The Eye of the
Needle* (1957), although I'm certainly grateful for the
very funny "Bartail Cock." Anyway here is one of his
civilized, classical, readable poems:

> The street-sounds of Delhi, the swirl
> Of colour and caste, endless and random,
> Did not disturb him as he sat on the ground
> In the small circle of his skill.
> A green bird perched on his forefinger.
> He threw a seed in the air, and the quick wings
> Flashed upward till beak caught the tiny prize
> Flew for an instant freely overhead
> An age-old anecdote of India
> Then, folding, fell to sudden stop
> Upon the waiting hand.
> The bird was safe again. A small green bird.
> One day I tossed into the living air
> Something you rose to take for nourishment,
> Something that bore you upward and beyond,
> But I had folded both my hands away
> And saw you fading, fading in the sky.

REVIEW OF *SELECTED POEMS*

CHESTER DUNCAN

Mr. Frank Scott's own selection of 115 of his poems . . .
has more range, more skill, more taste, and more wisdom
than any number of new volumes being published, with
some prolificacy, by the numerous talented, inexperienced,
and raw young poets of Canada. Mr. Scott is certainly not

From "New Canadian Poetry" by Chester Duncan. From *Canadian
Dimension*, Vol. 5 (April-May 1968), 39-40. Copyright 1968 by *Canadian Dimension*. Reprinted by permission of the author and *Canadian
Dimension*.

a great poet, but he is an interesting, readable, and mostly very polished one. His poetry is available to the liberal, intellectual mind on its own level and does not demand some special, snobbish, woozy enthusiasm, which probably in most cases means that one is a drinking-partner, a slightly less gifted fellow-poet, or a smiling hanger-on.

The range of Mr. Scott's writing does not refer only to subjects (he is very well-read and perceptive), but also to style. About 20 of the poems are, as a type, either imagist or metaphysical. The trouble with the metaphysical ones is that, instead of being brilliant and daring in their free-wheeling intellectuality and learning (like Donne), they tend to be careful, contained, and wryly witty (like A. J. M. Smith). But they are not careful out of mere formal principle; they care about communicated sense. In their nice phrasing and studious exactness, the imagist poems are just good as H.D.'s. However, they are not sufficiently different from H.D.'s or Ezra Pound's brief snaps, and so they seem, with all their quality, old-fashioned. Perhaps this is because the phrasing is generally quietly competent rather than inevitable. In this group one rarely comes across the winding strength and individuality of this (from "Autumnal") :

> Death curves most carefully from
> the sky in this season
> To lay a memory at the roots of
> trees.

they are often surrounded by a writing too ordinary to be quite good enough. In this case the two preceding lines are:

> October is the month of dead leaves falling
> Beautifully to lie upon grey rock and ground

The next group of poems is more concerned specifically with Canada now or lately and the dilemma or challenge of being a Canadian. Such poems are often journalistic,

and although one wishes that there were in existence a
tremendous body of such pieces from sensitive and culti-
vated Canadian minds, they do tend to become dated, and
to seem more superficially topical with the passing years.
There is hardly any proper satire in Canadian poetry; the
writers are generally too romantically self-obsessed to be
of any use in this department. Therefore it is fine that we
have at least one poet who can operate with considerable
passion in this field. Even if "The Canadian Authors
Meet," in its adolescence and unkindness, gets worse and
worse with the years, and "Saturday's Sundae" is like last
year's pop, Mr. Scott's intelligence and anger and bite are
wholly adequate to the succinct perception of "Brébeuf
and His Brethren" and "Examiner," in which:

> Each brick-walled barracks
> Cut into numbered rooms, blackboarded,
> Ties the venturing shoot to the master stick;
> The screw-desk rows of lads and girls
> Subdued in the shade of an adult—
> Their acid subsoil—
> Shape the new to the old in the ashen garden.

And "Audacity" and "A Lass in Wonderland" have in a
lively form the strangely long-absent humour (as dis-
tinct from gross, coterie haw-hawing) in Canadian poetry.
All these poems are worth reading, though some of them
are a little more angry than effective, a little more naive
than innocent, and a little more polemical than wise.
"Treasure in Heaven," however, is very fine, and as criti-
cism rampant, "All the Spikes But the Last" is smashing.

> Where are the coolies in your poem, Ned?
> Where are the thousands from China who swung
> their picks with bare hands at forty below?

Towards the end of this section there are some transla-
tions of French-Canadian poetry, translations so brilliant
that they are poems themselves.

The third section of the book is mostly given up to the subject of war.

> Move out and let me in
> Cry the nations, one to one,
> Your God's kingdom is down,
> Now it is my God's turn.

These poems are generally less than completely successful, though they are thoughtful and sometimes passionate. But here is a case where the subject is too vast for the diction to avoid generality or banality. Could it be that Mr. Scott's "Creed":

> The world is my country
> The human race is my race,

is better reversed, as far as art is concerned?

The last group of poems have to do with what in life is perhaps closest to the author: his art and his love (for sweethearts, heroes, and friends). Again, though some of the diction can be off-centre and the unity lost, there are enough good examples of things well and delicately done to give one renewed confidence in the older generation of Canadian writers. Part of the reason for this elevation undoubtedly is the contrast these poems afford to the flood of dithyrambic nonsense by which many young Canadian poets are attempting to prove their freedom and vitality. Such abandonments are a striking contrast to the artistic lyricism of Mr. Scott's "Departure," and beautiful "Heart" and—strangely enough the only poem in the book which one would ever want to set to music—"Caring."

A POET OF THE MIDDLE SLOPES

ROBIN SKELTON

At a time when frenetic symbolism and rhetorical gesti-
culation are running neck and neck with pseudo-imagist
reportage and structureless colloquialism in the race to-
wards a Canadian Parnassus, it is enormously rewarding
to turn one's glasses on a poet of a different colour, and
one whose measured steady progress has been unattended
by ballyhoo and self-dramatization. F. R. Scott's *Selected
Poems* brings together the best work of over forty years,
and the result is impressive.

Mr. Scott has not chosen to date the poems in his col-
lection, so that it is impossible, without doing a good deal
of research, to discuss the poems chronologically. I am
sure this is deliberate; what matters about poetry is not
its development but its identity. This book represents, not
a history, but a poetic personality, and the varying view-
points and tones are better seen as complementary por-
tions of one pattern than as stages upon a journey.

As one reads the book the pattern emerges very clearly.
It is, I think, the pressure of intelligence that dominates
and moulds Mr. Scott's poetry. This intelligent, rigorous,
even sceptical, approach to experience is most obvious in
the satirical poems, of course, for there the intelligence
must have the last incisive and derisory word. It is also,
however, present in the most lyrical and most symbolic
poems. Thus, when we read the final stanza of "Old Song":

> only a moving
> with no note
> granite lips
> a stone throat

"A Poet of the Middle Slopes" by Robin Skelton. From *Canadian
Literature*, No. 31 (Winter 1967), 40-5. Copyright 1967 by *Canadian
Literature*. Reprinted by permission of the author and *Canadian
Literature*.

while we are affected by the associate power of the imagery, we are equally moved by the economy and rigour of language; the poem displays its decisiveness as an essential part of its perception. Thus again in "Trans Canada" the implications of the opening images are witty as well as sensually vivid.

> Pulled from our ruts by the made-to-order gale
> We sprang upward into a wider prairie
> And dropped Regina below like a pile of bones.

If, here, the implications of the ascent of the spirit from the body, and the hint at the hackneyed after-life image of happy hunting grounds, have, like the "made-to-order gale," sardonic overtones, this does not in any way destroy, but rather enriches the validity of the speaker's emotions. Scott, like Donne, like Carew, and like Marvell, speaks as a complete man; his passions involve his intelligence, and his intelligence gives rise to passion.

It is, perhaps, characteristic of any poet addicted to the precise counterpointing of intelligence and passion that he should also be inclined towards neatness of form. Scott has handled most kinds of verse in his time, and his sense of form is such that he can make the most of free as well as of highly disciplined patterns. He knows the possibilities of colloquial ease as well as he knows the opportunities of formal rhetoric. Thus, looking through his work one can gather examples of technical expertise in almost every manner.

Compare for example the deftly Whitmanesque opening of "Audacity" with the gnomic traditionalism of "Advice".

> They say we lack audacity, that we are middle class,
>   without the adventurousness that arises from the
>   desperation of the lower classes or the tradition of
>   the upper classes.
> They say we are more emphatically middling than any
>   country west of Switzerland, and that boldness and
>   experiment are far from our complacent thoughts.

But I say to you, they do not know where to look, and
    have not the eyes to see.
For audacity is all around us,
Boldness sits in the highest places,
We are riddled with insolence.   *Audacity*

    Beware the casual need
    By which the heart is bound;
    Pluck out the quickening seed
    That falls on stony ground.

    Forgo the shallow gain,
    The favour of an hour.
    Escape, by early pain
    The death before the flower.   *Advice*

This type of control leads sometimes to a self-conscious-
ness that militates against passion and over-emphasizes the
virtue of order. Certainly there are very few instances of
emotional excess, and even the visionary poems rather sug-
gest a disciplined contemplation than a blinding illumina-
tion on the road to Emmaus.

This is, perhaps, healthy. The Romantic heresy that
the philosophic importance of an experience is the greater
the nearer it gets to hysteria finds no support in F. R.
Scott; he is clearly inclined to reverse Blake's dictum and
say "Bless braces, damn relaxes." Nevertheless, there is
great emotional power in many of his poems; the power
is expressed by the tautness of the verse and the poised
tension of the language, thus "Coil" begins:

    Coil is a tense
    a caged thing
    coil is a snake
    or a live spring

Against the tension, however, is balanced a sense of calm
and a feeling for slow organic movement. Thus "Depar-
ture" concludes:

    We shall find, each, the deep sea in the end,
    A stillness, and a movement only of tides

> That wash a world, whole continents between,
> Flooding the estuaries of alien lands.
> And we shall know, after the flow and ebb,
> Things central, absolute and whole.
> Brought clear of silt, into the open roads,
> Events shall pass like waves, and we shall stay.

Mr. Scott's imagery is rarely very novel, though it is almost invarably appropriate. He deals in images of the natural landscape and the seasons more than in those of the city, though his satirical poems are inclined to be both urban and urbane. The third stanza of "Boston Tea Party 1940" runs:

> The Harvard pundit's tea is brought
> Amid the ample female forms.
> He quits his crevices of thought
> To taste the soft and simpler norms . . . .

This, in syntactical structure and in cadence, is very close to Eliot, and I am sure the closeness is intentional. Here, however, as in some other cases, the result is rather a predictability of tone than an enriching ambiguity of reference. A poem that operates simultaneously in terms of two sensibilities, one ostensible and one implied by allusion or pastiche, requires an all-embracing, all-including originality of vision if it is not to become merely a pleasing game. It must be admitted that many of Mr. Scott's poems become games. Sometimes these are delightful, and yet such trivia as "The Canadian Authors Meet" and "Saturday Sundae" impose a superficiality upon the total persona of the book; the former jibe has point and still applies, but even here there are moments of mere facetiousness. "Saturday Sundae" is worse, being both arch and insensitive.

> Him of the front-flap apron, him I sing,
> The counter-clockwise clerk in underalls.
> Swing low, sweet chocolate, Oh swing, swing,
> While cheek by juke the jitter chatter falls.

The sensibility portrayed by the poem's speaker seems to me to be even less attractive than that of the world he mocks.

> My brothers and my sisters, two by two,
> Sit sipping succulence and sighing sex.
> Each tiny adolescent universe
> A world the vested interests annex.

There is an element of potential pathos here which undermines the whole poem, and makes the final verse appear both imperceptive and heartless.

The satirical poems of F. R. Scott, though much praised, seem to me too often to lack the hunger after the ideal, which animates the best satirists, whether of the radical or other persuasion. There is more cleverness than vehemence about them; they relate to the great satires as the grotesqueries of Leech relate to those of Goya.

It is, perhaps, by way of the satires that I find myself coming to a conclusion about Scott's work. He is a splendid versifier, an intensely intelligent writer, a wit, and a man of deep feeling; nevertheless, though his stated opinions are often radical, liberal, and sophisticated, his modes of operation are so dependent upon already established modes and attitudes that poetically (and in the context, not of Canada, but of the English-speaking world) he must be regarded as a conservative. Nevertheless on the Canadian scene he is an important figure, he represents emotional discipline, intelligence, and craftsmanship, and must be reckoned one of our four or five finest living poets. His work may not place him alongside the greatest of the twentieth-century poets of England and America, but poets should be judged by their excellences not by their limitations, and Scott has made a number of poems that ensure his survival down the years. He may not have reached the highest peak of Parnassus, but he is assured of a place upon the middle slopes. Only a very few can ever hope to climb farther.

F. R. SCOTT AND SOME OF HIS POEMS

A. J. M. SMITH

In Frank Scott we have a figure whom some Carlyle of Canada's second century might write about as The Hero as Canadian Poet or perhaps more soberly as The Poet as Man of Action. Politician, lawyer, teacher, scholar, and public figure. F. R. Scott has been in the forefront of the battle for civil liberties and social justice in Canada. He was one of the doctors presiding over the births of the CCF and the New Democratic Party; he fought and won the legal battles against the padlock law of Premier Duplessis and against the censorship of *Lady Chatterley's Lover*; he has written studies of Canada's constitution, has been Dean of Law at McGill, and is at present a member of the Royal Commission on Bilingualism and Biculturism. And he has, since his early days as a law student at McGill, been a poet.

The main function of a poet, of course, is to write poems, and Scott has been doing that steadily for more than three and a half decades. But his energy, his generous good will, and his natural self-assertiveness that makes him an inevitable and stimulating leader, were thrown into the battle for the new poetry in Canada as soon as it was joined in the mid-twenties. The now classic satire "The Canadian Authors Meet" was one of his first shots, while his social and editorial participation in the doings of the *Preview* group and the encouragement he has given to other poets in Montreal have kept up the good work to the present moment. There is hardly a poet in Canada who has not, passing through Montreal, made his pilgrimage to Clarke

"F. R. Scott and Some of His Poems" by A. J. M. Smith. From *Canadian Literature*, No. 31 (Winter 1967), 25-35. Copyright 1967 by *Canadian Literature*. Reprinted by permission of the author and *Canadian Literature*.

Avenue, Westmount, and been royally entertained and stimulated with wise and witty talk about poetry and poets; and all of them from the early days of Leo Kennedy, Abe Klein, and myself, through the time of Patrick Anderson, John Sutherland, P. K. Page and the rest, to the overlapping and heterogeneous groups that might include Louis Dudek, Ralph Gustafson, Irving Layton, Doug Jones, and John Glassco, felt the charm, energy and good sense that animated Frank Scott and make him one of the leaders in every group.

Ralph Gustafson has expressed in an appropriate and witty piece of verse a judgment that I think every one of the poets I have named would agree is just:

> To say
> that this man is fantastic
> is to be
> Frankly wrong.
> Real
> is the right root
> for him.
> He bears history,
> the lakes
> he dives under,
> the cold hard sun
> he walks in,
> Canada perhaps. . . .
>
> Praise
> he goes into,
> padlocks
> he gets well out of
> and piety. . . .
>
> Mortality
> moves him,
> he goes for wrong-doing,
> never lets bad enough
> alone. . . .

Words
he gets the wear out of . . .
buries with respectable honour
goes
Scott-free.

"He bears history,/the lakes/he dives under . . ." These
lines will take us into the first poem in Scott's new book,
"Lakeshore," one of the finest and most characteristic
pieces in the collection.

It will serve as a gateway through which to enter into an
examination of some of his most striking themes and inter-
esting techniques.

Its theme is Man's history, which extends back into pre-
history and before man. Its unifying symbol is water as the
source of life. The poem establishes through a specific
concrete personal experience a contact in awareness with
biological history, stretching back to the primordial begin-
nings of life and all around to the earthbound mechanical
now of "a crowded street."

By the edge of a lake, the poet—or, better, the sensuous
mind that is the protagonist of so many of Scott's meta-
physical lyrics—contemplates water, earth, and sky. There
is first "the bevelled edge of land," then "the fretted sands"
that the eye follows as they "go slanting down through
liquid air." Now the regard is fixed on stones below the
surface of the water and held too at the surface where the
stones seem to be

Floating upon their broken sky
All netted by the prism wave
And rippled where the currents are.

This is exact, clear, and elegant. There is a seventeenth-
century grace about these opening lines. One thinks of
Cowley's praise: "His candid style like a clean stream does
slide." It is a style that admits, indeed invites, Wit—as we

see in the next couple of stanzas. The poet (Man-and-Mind) peers into the water.

> I stare through windows at this cave
> Where fish, like planes, slow-motioned, fly
> Poised in a still of gravity . . .

The windows are the surface of the water and the surfaces of the eyes. Note also the hushed gravity of the last line and the gentle punning on *still*.

But the most striking object that confronts the poet is his own reflection.

> I am a tall frond that waves
> Its head below its rooted feet
> Seeking the light that draws it down
> To forest floors beyond its reach
> Vivid with gloom and eerie dreams.

At the beginning of the fourth stanza the sensuous mind dives down into the depths of the water and into the pre-racial aeons of the past, and for the four next stanzas we become, like the diver, liquid and loosed and silent, "Stroked by the fingertips of love,"

> Too virginal for speech or sound
> And each is personal and laned
> Along his private aqueduct.

But this return to the all-embracing primordial womb can be only a momentary glimpse of a long-lost freedom, a long since forfeited harmony with our environment.

> Too soon the tether of the lungs
> Is taut and straining, and we rise
> Upon our undeveloped wings
> Toward the prison of our ground
> A secret anguish in our thighs
>
> And mermaids in our memories.

> This is our talent, to have grown
> Upright in posture, false-erect,
> A landed gentry, circumspect,
> Tied to a horizontal soil
> The floor and ceiling of the soul;
> Striving, with cold and fishy care
> To make an ocean of the air.

The physical and sensuous exactness of the beginnings of the first of these two stanzas is admirable, as is the emotional and imaginative rightness of the end. The witty implications in naming our arms "our undeveloped wings" should not go without notice either. In the next stanza, the aptness of the joke in calling mankind "a landed gentry" adds to the laughter of the mind which it is one—though only one—of the functions of this poem to provoke.

But it is not with laughter, however philosophical, that the poem ends, but with wonder.

> Sometimes, upon a crowded street,
> I feel the sudden rain come down
> And in the old, magnetic sound
> I hear the opening of a gate
> That loosens all the seven seas.
> Watching the whole creation drown
> I muse, alone, on Ararat.

Here, at the threshold of his book, Scott moves from the poetry of concrete images through wit and metaphysical imagination to myth and magic. A long cool dive into Lake Massawippi and the poet comes up with a rich hoard of racial memories, dreams and aspirations. All are perfectly fused: earth, water, air; science and mythology; mermaids, Venus, Noah; the I and All-Mankind; a crowded street and "the water's deepest colonnades."

"Lakeshore" is an excellent starting point for a consideration of Scott's non-satirical poetry. The themes and the motives of many of his most completely articulated poems are seen in it at their clearest and most direct. The fascination with water, as element and as a symbol; the identification of the poet's Self with Man and of the sensuous perceptive physical being with Mind; and the inescapable tendency to identify or interchange the language and imagery of science (especially biology, geology and psychology) with the language and imagery of religion: all of these are here. And they are to be found also, in varying degrees and proportions, in such deeply felt and intellectually stimulating poems as "Paradise Lost," "Eden," "Journey," "My Amoeba is Unaware," and the best of the pieces on India and the Far East—"Bangkok," "Water," "A Grain of Rice," and "On the Death of Gandhi."

"Lakeshore" may also serve as an exemplar both of the "candid" style derived from Imagism and of the witty metaphysical style that, without being in the least derivative, recalls Marvell and Waller—or, if you prefer, Auden. Some of the earliest poems dating from the days of the *McGill Fortnightly Review* already have a simplicity of language and an exactness of imagery which are the first fruits of conscious discipline, control, and humility. Little pieces like "North Stream" and "Snowdrift" or the much later haiku "Plane Landing in Tokyo" exhibit these qualities in miniature splendour.

A pure and naked perception alone could not, of course, satisfy Scott for more than a moment, and most of his poems that start out as an image soon become images, and perceptions soon become concepts and blossom in metaphor, analogy and conceit. Mind comes flooding in.

Many of the early very simple verses grouped near the beginning of *Selected Poems* are nevertheless quite delightful, though their importance perhaps is mainly historical (they date from the mid-twenties) and technical (they show Scott's later style beginning to form). "New Names" develops in a personal and indeed almost rapturous way the old thesis that writers as different as Mrs. Traill and Mr. Douglas Le Pan have united in expressing—that Canada is a country without a mythology. Scott suggests we must make our own anew. "Old Song" finds and expresses an austere cadence in the almost-silence of the northern wilderness:

> far voices
> and fretting leaves
> this music the
> hillside gives
>
> but in the deep
> Laurentian river
> and elemental song
> for ever
>
> a quiet calling
> of no mind
> out of long aeons
>
> .   .   .   .   .   .
>
> granite lips
> a stone throat

Here we are back to the purest imagism and a style that is the ultimate in simplicity and suggestiveness. This poem has a theme and a style that are irresistibly appealing to the Canadian poet, as new poets like Bowering and Newlove show as clearly as E. J. Pratt or W. W. E. Ross. Here, as in "Lakeshore," we have the sense of vast distances in space and time and a view of geological prehistory that goes back even farther than the ages of man-as-fish.

Another poem that rises naturally out of such telescopic probings into the geologic and biologic past and therefore has affinities with "Lakeshore" and "Old Song" is the strange meditation called "Mount Royal." This is a Pratt poem with a difference. One thinks of the vivifying dynamism of the description of the Laurentian Shield in "Towards the Last Spike." Here time is speeded up: the Mountain rises out of the sea; the sea subsides, leaving its deposit of silt and shells; Man walks and builds his muddled cities "where crept the shiny mollusc," and the poet or poet-mind observes it all.

> Where flowers march, I dig these tiny shells
> Once deep-down fishes safe, it seemed, on sand. . . .

The joke about the fishes building on sand and thinking themselves safe alerts us to the fact that irony and satire are this poet's chosen weapons. The satire here is directed against man's vanity, pride, and blind self-confidence as in Hardy's lines on the loss of the *Titanic*, where dim moon-eyed fishes stare at the mighty wreck and query "What does this vaingloriousness down here?" The situation is reversed in "Mount Royal." It is the fish who have been stranded and passed by. Now they are cited as an object lesson that suburban and commercial man, who builds his villas on the reclaimed island of the mountain, fails to heed—blindly and foolishly, it is implied, since the forces of atomic destruction are to hand. The poem ends in angry scorn.

> Pay taxes now,
> Elect your boys, lay out your pleasant parks,
> You gill-lunged, quarrelsome ephemera!
> The tension tightens yearly, underneath,
> A folding continent shifts silently
> And oceans wait their turn for ice or streets.

There is a curious consequence of this geologic view that we can observe in some of Scott's most characteristic poems. He is a man capable of—indeed unable to refrain from—taking long views, both backwards into the past and forward into the future, an idealist in the popular sense of the word. Both in his political life as a socialist and his literary life as a poet he welcomes the new, the just, and the generous—and always in the broadest and most generous terms. Poems that embrace vast cosmic distances, both of space and time, lend themselves to thinking in abstractions. There is world enough and time for all the great abstractions to come into being, to evolve and grow, to change, to grow old, and perhaps to die. The good ones we must cultivate, preserve, and nourish; the bad ones we must kill.

There is a very peculiar class of poems in which these consequences of taking large views are quite explicit. Some of its members are "Creed," "Conflict," "Dialogue," "Degeneration," poems concerned with War or with Love, and a remarkable series of what for want of a better name I will call "defining" poems — among them "Memory," "Heart," "Was," "Caring," and (with a difference) "Stone." Let us look at one or two of them.

"Conflict" is a rather Emersonian poem on the tragic paradox of war. It develops the thesis that men on both sides in any conflict fight for the good they know and die with equal courage for the opposite sides of truth:

> When I see the falling bombs
> Then I see defended homes.
> Men above and men below
> Die to save the good they know. . . .

> Pro and con have single stem
> Half a truth dividing them. . . .

> Persecution's cruel mouth
> Shows a twisted love of truth. . . .

Here speaks the defender of unpopular causes, the idealist who loves the abstract and the universal. It is the wide application of unparticularized truth that such a poetry seeks to secure. Universals and abstractions are employed with the confidence born of an utter faith in their reality and validity. Such words as *good, wrong, bravery, love, truth, prison, ghetto, flag, gun, rack, rope, persecution, sacrifice*, whether abstractions or collective symbols, are made to glow with the vitality of an individual existence— or are used as if they did so glow.

How this is done, the eight quatrains entitled "Dialogue" may demonstrate. In structure and language this poem is as taut and concentrated as "Conflict," but its movement is in the reverse direction—from sensation and particularity (from the concrete, that is) to the universal, a universal which is equated with the spiritual—"spirit takes communion/From every living touch." The progression is straightforward. "Sense is more than mortal." Our bodies are the gateway to a supra-sensual world. Eye, ear, and hand contribute to the synthesis of a new form "to house a new conception."

> Desire first, then structure
> Complete the balanced picture.
> The thought requires the form.

The poem's rhetoric is serpentine, for we have now reached —this is the fifth of eight stanzas—the point where the poem begins:

> The hour is ripe for union,
> And spirit takes communion
> From every living touch.

The end in the last two stanzas is surprising and unheroic. The serpent cannot rear back and strike; instead it sinks down and seems to collapse.

> For us, how small the power
> To build our dreams a tower
> Or cast the molten need.
> For us, how small the power.

> So few, so worn, the symbols.
> No line or word resembles
> The vision in its womb.
> So few, so worn, the symbols.

Truth, not wishes, hopes, or evasions, is the business of poetry; and this poem would be a lesser one if it ended any other way.

What is needed always is a new language, new images, and a new technique. Scott has been trying all his life—and sometimes with heartening success—to find these. Some of his notable successes are moving love poems that have been placed in this collection immediately after "Dialogue." Their newness and hence their effectiveness lies in nothing more strange than an absolute fidelity to the occasion and the emotion that has brought them into being. One, called "Meeting," begins like this:

> If what we say and do is quick and intense,
> And if in our minds we see the end before starting,
> It is not fear, but understanding that holds us.

Here the conciseness of the syntax contributes potentialities to the meaning. It is not fear that holds us apart but understanding that holds us together.

Other poems that approach or achieve the new style are "Will to Win"—a deceptively light and witty *jeu d'esprit* in which the lightness enables the poet to keep control of the situation and the wit serves to define it; "Vision"—beautifully rhymed quatrains in which the "newness" or rightness comes from the clarity with which the sharp edge of every idea is defined: and "A l'Ange Avantgardien"—the explicit statement of a romantic view of poetic creation according to which the emphasis must always be on the making never on the made.

One of the most striking paradoxes of Scott's poetic life is that the ceaseless flow of energy which throws up poems of all kinds and in all modes should nevertheless be able to shape them with extreme care, whether the work in hand is a piece of impressionistic and typographical experiment or a closely knit web of thought, like the fine late poem "Vision"—a true metaphysical lyric that begins:

> Vision in long filaments flows
> through the needles of my eyes.
> I am fastened to the rose . . .
> I am clothed in what eye sees.

and ends:

> Tireless eye, so taut and long,
> Touching flowers and flames with ease,
> All your wires vibrate with song
> When it is the heart that sees.

Here is song that is as well written as prose—a poem that reiterates the validity of the "candid" style of "Lakeshore" and the earlier imagist pieces.

This style is seen at its most purely intellectual in what I have called the "defining" poems—lyrics that perhaps have developed out of Scott's training as a lawyer. Lawyers, like poets, are involved with words, with definitions and with subtle quibbles. Some of these pieces, as for example "Memory," are apt and ingenious metaphor:

> Was is an Is that died
>   in our careless hands
> and would not stay
>   in its niche of time.

> We crumble all our nows
>   into the dust of Was . . .
> forgetting Was

>   cannot be shaken off
>   follows close behind
>   breathes down our neck . . .

> One day we shall look back
>   into those staring eyes
> and there will be nothing left but
>   Was.

Another "defining" poem of the same sort is the one beginning "Caring is loving, motionless," but the lines entitled "Stone" show an interesting difference. In these what is being defined is not an abstraction or a state but an object, a solid item, "a still of gravity." The method is entirely different from that of imagism. The purpose of an imagist poem is to perceive and to present perception, but here we go further in an effort to grasp the idea of the thing and of its place in history. The motion too is just the reverse of that in "Was," where an abstraction was made concrete; here a concretion is seen in the light of thought—the remarkable thing being, however, that the thought is made to seem to radiate from the stone itself:

> A stone is a tomb
> with the door barred.
>
> A still picture
> from a flick of motion.
>
> A stone is a closed eye
> reflecting what it saw. . . .

In these distichs we come back to the sense of time in which Scott is so deeply immersed that it recurs in poem after poem. Here the mind moves from the glacial epochs of prehistory to the bursting stone that falls on Hiroshima.

Perhaps in coming to a close I should return to the personal. But actually I have not been away from it. The old dictum that the style is the man has never been more clearly illustrated than in the poetry of F. R. Scott. All his poems, from the gayest and lightest expression of delight in life through his pointed and savage satires to the profound lyrics I have been mainly considering, are informed and qualified by a sense of responsibility and an inescapable sincerity, which is serious but never solemn and rich without ostentation.

4. A. J. M. Smith

A. J. M. SMITH AND THE POETRY OF PRIDE

E. K. BROWN

It is eight years since the first appearance of a group of Mr. Smith's poems within the covers of a book. In the anthology *New Provinces* were twelve of his pieces, varying in their force and beauty from the sharp packed metaphysical imagery in "The Two Sides of a Drum"—

> that country under dream
> Where Eternity and Time
> Are the two sides of a drum

—to the cool conversational manner of Kenneth Fearing in "News of the Phoenix"—

> They say the Phoenix is dying, some say dead.
> Dead without issue is what one message said,
> But that was soon suppressed, officially denied.

At last Mr. Smith has brought out a collection of his own. My first feeling, at the mere sight of the book, was one of disappointment. It is a little book; it holds but thirty-nine poems, spread over about as many pages; and among the thirty-nine are the twelve from *New Provinces*, and others well known to the readers of more recent anthologies of Canadian verse. One had hoped for evidence of greater fertility. A poet who has added but twenty-seven pieces to his canon in seven years, and these the years from thirty-five to forty-two, is either the barren fellow that Johnson called Fielding, or else a most exigent critic.

"A. J. M. Smith and the Poetry of Pride" by E. K. Brown. From *Manitoba Arts Review*, 4 (Spring 1944), 30-32. Reprinted by permission of the estate of E. K. Brown.

It is an exigent temperament that this collection reveals, even a haughty temperament. In one of the most admirable poems, Mr. Smith espouses the "cold goddess Pride" and announces that it is to the "barren rock" he addresses his "difficult lonely music." In another, his most explicit exercise in criticism, he counsels a younger writer to aim at achieving the effect

> of a hard thing done
> Perfectly, as though without care.

The tone of that, as well as the idea, recalls the elder Yeats, to whom, in a memorial essay, Mr. Smith paid significant tribute, speaking of him as an "eye made aquiline by thought." Well, Mr. Smith, too, is aquiline, and it is temperament as much as thought, as it was with Yeats, that has made him so.

The eagle's vision is in that picture of the Canadian landscape called "The Lonely Land." This is a scene girt with sharp jagged firs and pines that a ceaseless wind has bent, spume is blown high in the air, and at the centre are wild ducks calling to each other in "ragged and passionate tones." The essence is stirringly caught in these lines:

> a beauty
> of dissonance
> this resonance
> of stony strand,
> this smoky cry
> curled over a black pine
> like a broken
> and wind-battered branch
> when the wind
> bends the tops of the pines
> and curdles the sky
> from the north.

In this harsh world Mr. Smith takes an austere and intense delight. The natural setting for his beautiful "Ode: on the Death of W. B. Yeats" is almost the same. His

Ireland has nothing in common with George Moore's or
Elizabeth Bowen's: it is no place of soft contours, rich
greenery, and gentle rain; his Ireland is the bare hills and
rough coast of Synge, and of Yeats in his elder years. If a
tree is conceded blossoms, it is a twisted tree; if a white
swan flies through the poem, the air is cold, and the clouds
above upheave.

Almost equal severity stamps the religious poems with
which the collection closes. In 1936 religion was a minor
theme in Mr. Smith's work, it was scarcely more than an
armoury of imagery. Now it is almost in the dominant
place. The choice of religious topics is revealing: Good
Friday, Calvary, Christian death. A line or two here and
there is infused with gentleness:

> And His face was a faded flower
> Drooping and lost

but lines such as these are among the least successful in
the book. The main effect is that of the Bellini portrait
of Christ: haggard, stricken, at odds with life.

Mr. Smith's theory of poetry leaves an honoured place
for satire and light verse. In the introduction to his im-
portant anthology, *The Book of Canadian Poetry,* he quotes
with approval Mr. Auden's warning that it will "do poetry
a great disservice if we confine it only to the major expe-
riences of life." "Far West" is a lightly satirical suggestion
of a London girl's feelings as "among the cigarettes and
the peppermint creams" she enjoys a movie about cow-
boys. Most acrid are "On Reading an Anthology of Popu-
lar Poetry" and "Son-and-Heir." In these Mr. Smith's
disgust with bourgeois values has a searing strength. "Son-
and-Heir" is an arraignment of bourgeois civilization in
terms of the reveries an average bourgeois couple might
have as they plot the ideal future for the baby. The quality
of the reveries is cheap, but Mr. Smith would emphasize
not only the cheapness, but the danger of having reveries
at all. He is as much the foe of revery as Irving Babbitt.

I mention Babbitt because the enmity Mr. Smith holds to romanticism is as deep as Babbitt's: the drubbing he gives to the anthology of popular poetry shows this to be so. Most of his phrases of contempt in the poem upon it might be paralleled in Babbitt, except that Mr. Smith, as a poet, properly heightens the feeling. He speaks of the "sweet sweet songs," the "soft melodious screams," the "old eternal frog in the throat that comes with the words, "Mother, sweetheart, dog." I have spoken at such length of Mr. Smith's satiric poems because I think that they, more clearly than any others in the book, make plain the pride and severity of his temperament. Read first, they will help prepare one for the emotions that lie within and behind the more difficult and more important pieces.

That Mr. Smith is a difficult poet he would not himself deny. There are phrases here and there in the book to which I cannot assign a clear meaning. Why should Buffalo Bill be described as "toxic"? I assume that it is because from the screen he entices to reverie. I can offer no suggestion why politeness should be compared to a "mezzanine floor." But whatever the difficulties it presents, this collection demonstrates again and again not merely triumphant virtuosity, but perfect keeping between substance and form. It is a book in many manners, but one can see why there must be many.

A proud, hard, noble and intense book, *News of the Phoenix* makes one regret that Mr. Smith has not been more fertile, or, if he has kept much back, that he should not have given us some peeps into the laboratory in which he works his wonders.

ARTHUR SMITH

W. E. COLLIN

La poésie de A. J. M. Smith est une fine fleur de l'intellectualisme conscient de notre époque qui se distingue par certains procédés rhétoriques que nous appelons "métaphysiques" et par certaines attitudes que nous pouvons appeler philosophiques au sens large. Comme ces procédés et attitudes sont généralement caractéristiques de ce que nous appelons la "nouvelle poésie," nous devons découvrir la place de Smith dans ce courant poétique dont W. B. Yeats et T. S. Eliot sont les figures les plus marquantes.

Smith est né de parents anglais à Montréal en 1902. Au cours de ses études secondaires à l'Université McGill, il fut surtout intéressé par une série de cours sur la littérature anglaise du dix-septième siècle donnée par un Anglais qui aurait probablement mis dans ses mains des plaquettes de vers de Edith Sitwell et de T. S. Eliot. Pour l'obtention de sa maîtrise ès arts, il présenta une dissertation sur la poésie de W. B. Yeats. Grâce à une bourse, il se rendit ensuite à Edinburgh où il poursuivit ses études sous la direction du professor John Grierson, bien connu pour ses études sur John Donne, et, pour l'obtention du doctorat, il prépara une thèse sur les poètes religieux du dix-septième siècle. De retour en Amérique, Smith devint professeur à l'University of South Dakota et au Michigan State College, à Lansing. Ses premiers poèmes parurent dans *The McGill Fortnightly Review*, *The Canadian Mercury* et *The Canadian Forum*. Depuis, il a publié des poèmes dans des revues anglaises et américaines. En même temps que des poèmes de Finch, Kennedy, Klein, Pratt et F. R. Scott, une douzaine de ces poèmes furent réunis dans

"Arthur Smith" by W. E. Collin. From *Gants Du Ciel*, II (Spring 1946), 47-60. Reprinted by permission of the author.

une petite anthologie de la nouvelle poésie canadienne, *New Provinces, Poems of Several Authors* (1936), dont Smith lui-même, je crois, rédigea la preface. La Guggenheim Foundation lui accorda une bourse pour préparer une anthologie historique et critique, *The Book of Canadian Poetry*. En 1943, sous le titre *News of the Phoenix*, il publia un recueil assez complet de ses poèmes qui, jusque là, etaient dispersés dans les revues de poésie.

On verra que le style de Smith a son point de depart chez W. B. Yeats, Edith Sitwell et T. S. Eliot. Il y a une vingtaine d'années, Eliot fut lié au renouveau d'interêt pour les poètes "métaphysiques" anglais, aux symbolistes francais et au groupe de poètes anglais et américains qui se sont baptisés eux-mêmes les Imagistes. La recherche de l'étonnement par l'invention de nouvelles images, l'esthétique de la suggestion basée sur la métaphore et le symbole, les concetti, la juxtaposition d'images qui jurent, l'esprit, défini par Eliot comme "a tough reasonableness under the slight lyric grace," constituent l'héritage que des poètes comme Eliot ont laissé à des hommes comme Smith. Mais ce n'est que pour des fins d'analyse que nous séparons le style du sentiment auquel il est substantiellement uni dans la poésie de Smith. Le style et le sentiment sont une seule et même chose, une pensée est un sentiment, et leur identité est le signe de cette "sensibilité unifiée" que Eliot découvrait chez les poètes métaphysiques. Nous retrouvons chez Smith "cette appréhension sensible directe de la pensée, ou cette recréation de la pensée dans le sentiment" que Eliot découvrait chez Chapman et chez Donne. La difficulté que nous avons à comprendre la poésie de Smith vient de ce que les pensées et sentiments sont exprimés en images et en symboles. Et nous devons dégager à notre tour de ces symboles les pensées, sentiments et attitudes du poète. C'est lorsque nous nous engageons dans ce travail que nous apprécions une certaine qualité de cette poésie, une qualité "perdue" que Smith appelle vitalité.

Dans la préface de *New Provinces,* il écrivait: "Possédant un style plus libre et des formes plus élastiques, les modernistes recherchent un contenu qui puisse exprimer d'un manière plus vivante le monde qui les entoure. Cette recherche d'un nouveau contenu a été moins heureuse que celle des nouvelles techniques, et à la fin de la dernière décennie le mouvement moderniste avorta faute de direction. La poésie ne reflétait ainsi que le désoevrement du milieu social. En imposant au monde le besoin de sortir du chaos et de rétablir l'ordre, la dépression économique a libéré les énergies humaines en leur donnant un but positif. Le poète profite aujourd'hui de cette libération et des signes indiquent que la poésie anglaise et américaine contemporaine retrouve la vitalité qu'elle avait perdue."

Depuis ses débuts, Smith a été préoccupé du problème social-esthetique des relations de l'artiste au monde qui l'environne et nous réussirons peut-être à décrire l'évolution de l'attitude du poète devant ce problème. Dans ses premiers poèmes, sous l'influence de Yeats, Smith apparaît comme un artiste en quête de la beauté parfaite et de la sagesse absolue. Dans "Something apart," le sentiment d'isolement du poète, de séparation du monde, s'exprime en symboles naturels, c'est le cri d'un oiseau sauvage dans un monde statique, cristallin:

> the raucous bird was something apart,
> As alien from all these
> As the sorrow in my heart.

D'autres poèmes doivent leurs symboles — "flamme," "lampe," "ombres dans l'esprit mortel" et "tour" — à des poèmes de Yeats tels que "The Tower" et "The Phases of the Moon." L'homme dans la tour le long de la route de Connemara sur laquelle

> Benighted travellers
> From markets and from fairs
> Have seen his midnight candle glimmering,

possèdes les étranges connaissances d'une obscure race
arabe, celle des Judwalis, et comme il est né près de la
pleine lune, qui chez les Judwalis est signe de parfaite
subjectivité et de beauté parfaite, il représente l'âme sub-
jective se recherchant elle-même. La beauté parfaite et
la sagesse absolue se trouvent dans la pure subjectivité.
Comme Smith, l'artiste à la recherche de son âme où il
croit découvrir la beauté et la sagesse, se trouve habiter
Montréal, "The Moment and the Lamp" debute par ce
vers:

> There is a beacon on a mointain top.

Dans ce poème, "lampe," "étoile filante," "sorciers," "al-
chimistes," "la lueur tremblotante de la chandelle" et "le
flux universel" font écho aux préoccupations néo-plato-
niques de Yeats: si nous connaissions la lueur qui luit
dans l'esprit du poète, nous saurions ce qu'est l'homme et
comprendrions sa destinée—

> There might be comprehension in the sky—

car cette lueur est celle de la sagesse, qui transcende le
temps et le changement. La sagesse est un forme parfaite
de luminère, un "cube de lumière," "sculpte à même le
chaos" dans "For Ever and Ever, Amen":

> Lonely aloft in a turret
> Hewn of the bodiless night
> Sits one who out of chaos
> Has carved a cube of light.
>
> Bent double over his book
> What does he ponder there
> As quiet and lonely as a planet
> Hung in the silent air?
>
> Looking out he sees only dark,
> There is no one to look in;
> When a gust twists the flame of his candle
> Shadows swim with no fin.

Ces ombres sont des pensées éternelles dans l'esprit du poète solitaire où

> The Is is the same as the Will Be
> And both the same as before.

Dans "Flame and Fountain" le symbolisme émotionnel est développé: le poète ne souffre pas seulement de sa solitude dans un monde noir et laid, il souffre encore de la perte de la béatitude de l'enfance. L'enfance est un autre monde dont il se sent séparé, éloigné. La "flamme" de son esprit, "méditant sur le pourquoi et le comment et le d'où," brûle encore dans "le noir absolu" mais il y a aussie la "fontaine" de son coeur plein de désirs, "souffrant de l'absence de nombre de choses qu'il regrette—bonté et compréhension, étonnement" s'élevant "comme un fantôme dans l'après-midi fantomatique," se tenant "pâle et d'un air glacial devant les ténèbres." Les choses qu'il pleure sont celles de son enfance perdue, car ce crépuscule spectral et glacial est l'univers de Miss Sitwell où l'innocence de l'enfance est perdue, comme Smith nous le rappelle dans "A Hyacinth for Edith," un des poèmes dans lesquels il imite consciemment l'imagerie de bois verni des ballades de Miss Sitwell et dans lesquels il cherche à retrouver la joie extatique de l'enfance:

> Now that the ashen rain of gummy April
> Clacks like a weedy and stain'd mill
>
> . . . .
>
> I'll seek within the wood's black plinth
> A candy-sweet sleek wooden hyacinth—
> And in its creaking naked glaze,
> And in the varnish of its blaze,
> The bird of ecstasy shall sing again
>
> . . . .
>
> Till I am grown again my own lost ghost
> Of joy, long lost given up for lost,
> And walk again the wild and sweet wildwood
> Of our lost innocence, our ghostly childhood.

L'innocence, "the innocent wood," est opposée à la nature "dépravée," "another wood," dans "Ode: the Eumenides." Comment pouvons-nous retrouver la vallée enfantine de l'innocence? demande Smith.

> Betrayed by the bold front and the bright line
> How shall we return to the significant dark
> Of piety and fear
> Where Holiness smoothed our hair
> And Honour kissed us goodbye?

Nous avons un rendez-vous dans "l'ombre enchantée" où l'homme goûta pour la première fois du fruit de l'arbre défendu et où un châtiment terrible l'attend, personnifié, comme dans la mythologie grecque, sous le nom effroyable des Furies.

> We have a date in another wood,
> In the stifling dark, where the Furies are:
> The unravelled implacable host
> With accurate eyes levelled
> Wait in the enchanted shade,
>
> Where we spilled our bloodshot seed
> They wait, each patient ghost
> My ruined son.

Le phénix est un développement du symbole de la flamme. Cet oiseau fabuleux se consume lui-même; mais de ses propres cendres il renaît jeune et frais. C'est pourquoi le phénix est souvent considéré comme un symbole de l'immortalité. Il symbolise également un modèle, une personne d'une rare perfection. Dans "News of the Phoenix," Smith compare le poète au phénix, un esprit immortel ou une flamme vivante, dans un monde, non pas noir cette fois, mais vulgaire, prêt à accepter toute rumeur de la mort d'un esprit rare.

L'esprit de l'artiste, toujours à la recherche de la perfection et vivant partiellement dans l'éternité, se sent insatisfait aussi longtemps qu'il habite en ce monde. Ce thème est magnifiquement exprimé dans un hymne de six vers lents, "Beside one dead," dans lequel les symboles philosophiques et religieux, le Verbe et le Seigneur, se rencontrent et dans lequel l'esprit vivant, symbolisé par "le glaive," nous est montré atteignant le plénitude de la perfection après en avoir souffert la privation lorsqu'il était enfermé dans un corps. Ces vers lents, ces images antithétiques, si soigneusement choisies, si éloquentes dans leur silence solennel, ne sont pas seulement une anticipation de la perfection, mais ils sont eux-mêmes parfaits:

> This is the sheath, the sword drawn,
>   These are the lips, the Word spoken;
> This is Calvary toward dawn;
>   And this is the third day token—
> The opened tomb and the Lord gone;
>   Something Whole that was broken.

L'idée d'une nouvelle vie dans la mort est évoquée dans "Prothalamium" comme un sacrement béni du marriage de la poussière du poète avec la terre. Le désir de plénitude est appelé prière et exprimé d'une manière qui rappelle les miracles du moyen âge dans "Prayer at Midnight." Dans l'angoisse de la nuit spirituelle, "a dark boy at midnight probing a sore," le poète, un garçon dont tous les traits disent la joie perdue, ses membres vifs et ses joues rouges laissés derrière lui dans le sable, demande à reprendre pleine possession de ses forces et implore le Christ de lui donner la foi, la substance de choses invisibles, comme l'appelle saint Paul:

> Jesus, shew me thy grass, thy green,
> Else how shall I keep this thing I have not seen?

Ainsi l'artiste, en quête de perfection et de plénitude, est représenté comme le "Divin Insatisfait" dans un autre poème, "Like an old proud king in a parable." C'est là que la parabole d'un roi qui, afin de rester seul avec sa conscience, jeta son sceptre trompeur et sa couronne d'or, abandonna les courtisans serviles et la reine radoteuse, et se réfugia dans la solitude des rochers balayés par le vent

pour chanter aux rocs arides la musique difficile et soli-
taire dont son coeur était plein.

Le renoncement au monde est évoqué dans "Testament"
avec les mêmes images arides dont Eliot s'était servi dans
des poèmes comme "The Waste Land" et "The Hollow
Men" pour peindre la sécheresse spirituelle que sa généra-
tion connut après la première guerre mondiale. Dans le
langage du désert, le mot "chair" est un mirage auquel le
poète dit adieu de la main:

> I'm for the desert and the desolation.
> I have kissed my hands to distant trees
> And to the girls with pitchers
> Waiting at the well,
> And I am set upon a pilgrimage
> Seeking a more difficult beauty
> Unheartened by even the most faint mirage.

Cette prière, cette parabole, ce pèlerinage indiquent
une évolution de la technique poétique qui rapproche
Smith de ce parangon de la poésie intellectuelle qu'est
Mallarmé,[1] dont il se distingue principalement par la
nature religieuse de son ascétisme, car, évidemment, ce re-
noncement au monde, cette recherche de la plénitude, ce
désir de la perfection, cette foi en l'immortalité de l'esprit
humain, sont inséparables des formes religieuses dans les-
quelles elles sont exprimées. L'artiste qui prie pour la
plenitude s'adresse à son Dieu; lorsqu'il part en pèlerinage
à la recherche de la perfection, qui est Dieu. Nous sommes
donc en présence d'un aspirant à la perfection et d'un
Dieu de perfection. Nous pouvons trouver quantité de
noms divins dans *The Golden Bough* de Frazer, qui fut si
précieux pour Eliot; mais pour un chrétien la source de
la perfection est le Christ et celui qui y aspire, qui re-

---

[1]Un des *Interviews imaginaires* de Gide est intitule "Saint Mallarmé
l'Esoterique." "Persuadez-vous, remarque Gide, que Mallarmé, dans
son ésotérisme, rejoignait une ancienne tradition dont John Donne
en Angleterre et Maurice Scève en France furent d'illustres représen-
tants."

cherche la plénitude de la perfection, la beauté de la sainteté, est appelé mystique ou saint.

Eliot a parlé d'une "génération que commence à porter son attention sur un athlétisme, un entraînement, de l'âme aussi sévère et rigoureux que l'entraînement du corps d'un coureur." Le poème de Smith "The Offices of the First and the Second Hour" nous révèle les premiers exercises du poète dans cet athlétisme ou entraînement de l'âme dont le but est la perfection. Dans ce fragment nous avons l'Art poétique de Smith, la poésie de la Règle de saint Benoît:

WHAT IS THE OFFICE OF THE FIRST HOUR?

To abjure the kindness of darkness, humbly
To concede the irrelevant spite of the spirit,
The mightlike melancholy fleshcase, and the
Romantic unnecessary cape of the naked heart.

WHAT IS THE OFFICE OF THE SECOND HOUR?

Quietly to attend the unfolding light's stark
Patience, inhuman and faithful like a weed or a flower.
Empty of darkness and light.

La nuit est bienveillante parce qu'elle nous permet d'agir sans entrave, inaperçus, et nous devons abandonner la facile et agréable vie sensuelle de la chair que l'esprit méprise. Lorsque nous nous sommes dépouillés de cette vanité, de l'ignorance, de la vulgarité et de l'erreur, alors, au second stage, nous sommes dans l'attente de la lumière pénétrante de la vérité spirituelle, qui ne nous est pas encore révélée toutefois, car nous n'en sommes encore qu'au second stage de la perfection.

Ce que nous trouvons dans ce fragment, c'est la séparation de deux conceptions entièrement différentes de la nature de l'homme: la romantique ("fleshcase") et la religieuse ("inhuman and faithful"). Le penseur qui, de nos jours, a sérieusement médité sur ces deux conceptions opposées et qui a senti la grave nécessité de les distinguer, est T. E. Hulme. Hulme sentit la "nécessité urgente" de détruire le principe de continuité qui avait été mis à la mode et universellement appliqué au dix-neuvième siècle. "Certains domaines de la réalité diffèrent non relativement mais absolument. Il existe entre eux une réelle discontinuité." Il posait un vide entre la zone absolue de la religion et la zone essentiellement relative et non-absolue des choses humaines. Il rejetait le romantisme avec violence. "Le romantisme, dit-il, confound les choses humaines avec celles de Dieu, en ne les séparant pas clairement. Le principal reproche que nous puissions lui faire est de brouiller les grandes lignes des relations humaines en introduisant en elles la *Perfection* qui appartient en propre à ce qui dépasse l'homme." Il ajoute: "A la lumière de cette valeur absolue, l'homme est jugé comme essentiellement limité et imparfait. Il est atteint par le péché originel. S'il peut accomplir parfois des actes participent de la perfection, il ne peut jamais *être* lui-même parfait. . . . Il ne peut accomplir d'actions de valeur que par la discipline."[1] Dans ce travail de destruction, Hulme accomplissait en Angleterre un travail analogue à celui que des hommes comme Lasserre accomplissaient en France. Mais il ouvrait aussi une nouvelle voie à ses disciples. Eliot suivit Hulme et Smith suivit Eliot. Cette voie est celle de la perfection, de la chasteté et du renoncement. Rien d'imparfait ne satisfera Smith. Aucun poète ne se fit jamais une conception aussi haute de son art. Il ne fait absolument aucune concession à l'homme ordinaire. La sentimentalité, l'hypocrisie, la grandiloquence, tout élément populaire, tout lieu commun, ont été bannis de sa poésie; la relation entre le poète et son milieu, entre le poète et son Dieu, est, par une alchimie subtile, devenue symbole et parabole incarnés. L'intensité et la puissance des essences que sont ses poèmes sont inégalées dans notre poésie canadienne. Le seul poème que je connaisse qui puisse

---

[1] *Speculations.*

être placé aux côtes de ceux de Smith est un chef-d'oeuvre
de Kennedy, "Words for a Resurrection."

Pour parler comme Hulme, l'intensité de l'attitude
religieuse que s'exprime dans l'art de Smith "ne vient pas
de la jouissance de la vie mais de l'intuition de certaines
valeurs absolues." Mais pour apprécier pleinement l'in-
tensité et la puissance de l'art de Smith, nous devons
l'étudier d'un peu plus près. L'intensité, la vitalité et la
puissance qui nous émerveillent dans ces poèmes ne
résultent pas seulement de l'attitude qu'ils expriment mais
aussi des instruments d'expression: symboles, métaphores,
mots. Il y a, il n'en faut pas douter, une puissance qui
résulte de son renoncement au monde, mais sa puissance
artistique subtile résulte de l'usage qu'il fait de ses moyens
d'expression qui lui servent à exprimer ce refus du monde.
Telle est la puissance que nous sentons dans des expres-
sions comme celles que nous avons citées: "Flung hollow
sceptre and gilt crown away," "I'm for the desert and the
desolation," "the girls with pitchers waiting at the well,"
"unheartened by even the most faint mirage," "this is the
sheath, the sword drawn." Il y a aussi le pouvoir que ces
symboles ont de nous soumettre à une discipline sévère,
semblable à celle que le poète lui-même s'est imposée,
jusqu'à ce que nous ayions découvert leur rapport avec
son attitude et compris leur sens. De plus, il ya a une
puissance dans le mot austère, un pouvoir littéraire vital
d'évocation. Un exemple suffira. Avec le développement
de son symbolisme religieux, il etait naturel que Smith se
trouve en présence de la Passion de Notre-Seigneur et
identifie à la passion du Christ l'angoisse du poète perdu
dans le monde. Bien que, comme nous le verrons, ce ne
soit pas le sentiment dominant dans le poème "Good
Friday," c'est un des sentiments qui y sont exprimés et
son intensité vient de cette identification ("godhead in
human agony," "as Man to die") . Il y a aussi de la puis-
sance dans les métaphores austères ("His face was a faded

flower," "struck as with darts"). Et, enfin, il y a de la puissance dans les simples mots concrets:

> What answering meed of love
> Can finite flesh return
> That is not all unworthy of
> The God I mourn?

Quelle "meed" d'amour? *Meed*, un monosyllabe anglo-saxon qui nous apporte un echo des débuts de notre histoire poétique. Et quel est, en somme, le pouvoir que ces choses peuvent avoir sur nous? Voici: elles nous réduisent à un sentiment simple, élémentaire: exprimer le sentiment de notre indignité devant le Verbe incarné. Et c'est là l'angoisse essentielle de l'artiste; quelle que soit la discipline à laquelle il soumette son art, aussi près qu'il approche de son idéal, il se sentira toujours indigne de la perfection.

Une des choses les plus remarquables que le métaphysicien français Gabriel Marcel ait dites est la suivante: "Ce que j'ai aperçu en tout cas, c'est l'identité cachée de la voie qui mène à la sainteté et du chemin qui conduit le métaphysicien à l'affirmation de l'être; la nécessité surtout, pour une philosophie concrète, de reconnaître qu'il y a là un seul et même chemin."[1] Les attitudes et sentiments exprimés dans la poésie de Smith—foi en l'immortalité de l'esprit humain, nostalgie de l'innocence perdue, piété, sainteté et charité, renoncement au monde, désir de perfection, et l'angoisse de l'indignité—suffiraient à lui donner un sens à notre époque. "L'appréhension sensible directe de la pensée ou la recréation de la pensée dans le sentiment" que nous y trouvons lui donnerait une place enviable dans la tradition de Chapman, Donne, Yeats et Eliot. Mais le caractère distinctif de Smith au nombre des poètes métaphysiques, c'est, je crois, d'avoir aperçu que la voie du poète et celle du saint sont une seule et même voie. Tel est le signe auquel nous reconnaissons la "personnalité unifié" de Smith. La vérité essentielle de cette

---

[1] *Etre et Avoir.*

poésie réside dans l'identification de l'esprit du poète à l'esprit de Dieu. Et cette vérité essentielle est en elle-même un instrument, une flamme sainte qui purifie et révèle, qui polit les pensées et les sentiments jusqu'à ce qu'ils nous éblouissent et nous remuent profondément par leur splendeur. Car, comme cette vérité, cette poésie est immortelle. Le temps ne saurait émousser ses vers, le souffle du vulgaire ne saurait ternir son lustre.

AFTER STRANGE GODS

PADRAIG O BROIN

For the person living in Canada, there are two things he cannot be detached from—his Canadianism . . . invisible and often unconscious attachments . . . they condition the inevitable way in which emotion and thought rise out of sensibility.
                                                        A. J. M. Smith[1]

There are climates of opinion in which it is fashionable to decry nationalism, to deny its influence on and its importance for the creative writer—the only writer time remembers. As long ago as the thirties A. J. M. Smith attacked this concept of nationalism in literature. However, in an enthusiastic letter to *Canadian Forum* (XXIV [1944] 89) welcoming Patrick Anderson's "Poem on Canada," he seemed to change his mind and come down on the side of nationalism, regarding Anderson's poem as:

on a large and generous scale, and full of specific felicities that dazzle and satisfy. . . . Where . . . can we find writing whose substance and texture are more certainly Canadian than here?

"After Strange Gods" by Padraig O Broin. From *Canadian Author and Bookman*, 39 (Summer 1964), 6-8. Copyright 1964 by *Canadian Author and Bookman*. Reprinted by permission of *Canadian Author and Bookman*.
[1]"Eclectic Detachment: Aspects of Identity in Canadian Poetry." *Canadian Literature* 9 (Summer 1961), 12.

Three years later, however, Smith's attitude to that same poem seemed to indicate withdrawal of approval. He now felt merely that Anderson:

tried to be a national poet, notably in the interesting and important, though not completely successful "Poem on Canada." Perhaps I ought to say why I think this poem falls short of its promise . . . welcoming the first publication of the poem, I wrote: "Here we have a serious and exuberant writer coming to grips with the fundamental task of the Canadian poet—the examination of our cultural traditions and the definition of our selfhood—and doing so with an intensity and an imaginative insight . . . commensurate with the subject". In the main this is true, and it indicates why this is an important poem. But it [*sic* Smith's opinion] needs to be modified. I now think the subject is bigger than I then thought. And it is bigger than Anderson's fine poem.

Canadian Forum (**XXVI** [1947] 520)

The subject is indeed big, bigger than any man's poem is likely to be. But Anderson's was a worthwhile attempt at compassing Canada and Canadianism (the latter a somewhat scarce commodity in the early forties), and it is of some psychological interest to trace Smith's continued interest in, but changing opinion of a poem which has now worn well for twenty years. In editing the *Oxford Book of Canadian Verse* (1960) he watered down his earlier praise and murmured only that Anderson had "turned his attention with refreshing gusto to the problem of Canadian identity. His 'Poem on Canada' (1946) [sic] has much that is individual and penetrating" (*O.B.C.V.* xlvii). Such cavalier dismissal of "an important" poem would seem to indicate Smith's progressive detachment from the tap root that might have nourished his poetry.

This problem of nationality is one of special import to the writer, particularly the poet. If physically severed from his country, from the people, the place, the very air and soil and running water which were his birthright, can he, so cut off, more than exist? Can he create without constant recourse to his source?

One remembers a Thucydides, banished from Athens for an error of judgement in battle. In the long years abroad he wrote a history of the Peloponnesian War—in it, incidentally, recording without comment his own exile. With no emotion seeping through he looks back at his *polis*, recording her successes, her failures, her glory and her shame, with equal objectivity. Objective, yes; but all his subject, Athens.

One remembers the greatest writer the Western World has yet known in this era—banished from his homeland, looking back from Ravenna with heartsick longing for the Florence he would not see again. How Dante felt, all the literate world knows. Deprived of his own proper place, he equated himself almost with God. In place of Florence he created a universe, peopling it out of legend, literature, life: those whom he deemed his own, his country's, the Church's friends exalted; those whom he deemed their enemies, damned. And exalting one girl as no human has, before or since, honoured a woman, he welded the whole inchoate mass into a living unity rising through the Beatific to culminate in the Beatific Vision. Yet not even another universe and entry in some sort into heaven could assuage that tormented heart. Throughout Dante thought of, drew on his awareness of, wrote of, Florence incarnate in her daughter.

A more recent example is that Dubliner who, despite self-imposed exile from the town that made him, and despite its sometime censorship of his early work, all his life long wrote of and for that city.

Thucydides in exile remained an Athenian, Dante a Florentine, Joyce a Dubliner. They transcended nationality in its narrower sense to write as citizens of a world, but only because they remained local and individual. Writing primarily of and for their own people and out of their own blood and marrow, that very concentration of purpose ensured that what they so wrote should be for all men and all time. Athenian. Florentine. Dubliner. All with one thing in common: their cities were their work, their love, their true religion, their life. And through their cities they have become immortal as, through them, their cities too are immortalized.

That is the right way, the true way, the ideal for an exile. It is a far cry from this involvement with *polis, civitas, patria,* swelling until it involves all time and space, to the position of many a modern writer who holds no loyalty to place; who leaves one country to become a willing citizen of another: an Eliot to England, an Auden scrabbling for Yankee citizenship in the year of grace 1939:

> I sit in one of the dives
> On Fifty-Second Street
> Uncertain and afraid.
>
> —"September 1, 1939"

Arthur James Marshall Smith is not quite of either type. Although of English parentage, he was born in Montreal, 1902. There he attended McGill. He later studied in Edinburgh; and for at least twenty years has taught in the United States, first at Doane College, Nebraska, later at Michigan State University. While many verse writers who have come here from elsewhere rank, particularly in Smith's own anthologies, as Canadian, Smith reverses the process. The Yankees have not yet claimed him. Presumably taking "his personality and his Canadianism" with him, despite long foreign residence he sees himself as still Canadian; and as prolific critic and anthologist of Canadian verse, he is regarded here as a Canadian writer.

Is he so in fact? Has prolonged residence abroad had no influence on his work? How does he reconcile in heart and mind a foreign world and that Canada which for him should be earth's centre?

Take his *Collected Poems* (1962)—themselves printed in England. Unless one assumes the contents to be only the amount of verse a publisher was willing to risk money on, the title must imply that the book's hundred poems constitute what Smith wants to preserve as an integrated corpus. Most of it is early material—*News of the Phoenix* (1943), for instance, is reprinted entire, though the poems are not in their original order. This deliberate re-ordering into five sections supports the belief that the book contains what Smith would like to be judged by.

It cannot be denied that he is a poet. That knowledgeable critic E. K. Brown spoke of Smith's "Poetry of Pride" (*Manitoba Arts Review* 4 [Spring 1944] 30-32). *Collected Poems* opens on that note with what is, to judge from its frequent appearance, one of Smith's favourite poems, "Like an Old Proud King in a Parable." In this early poem he prays to lie

> . . . naked as a bridegroom by his bride,
> And let that girl be the cold goddess Pride.

Certainly a wish anyone worthy the name poet must echo. In a later poem, "Nightfall," he chooses that words be "crisp and sharp." This pride, this crispness and sharpness, run like an icicle through many of the better poems in the book, producing sometimes "The angular creaking note . . . From the cat-bird's ragged throat" (43); but more often lines that, like his "Mermaid,"

> . . . come where bubbles burst, crisp silver skins;
> Where the tall sun stands naked. . . . (42)

Much of this music of meaningful words comes from good exemplars. Smith's thesis for his McGill M.A. dealt with the early and middle Yeats, and "Like an Old Proud King . . ." for example, is reminiscent of the Yeats who wrote *Responsibilities* (1914). Smith took a doctorate at Edinburgh with a thesis on the seventeenth-century English religious poets. Both these influences, coupled with

that of the "metaphysical revolution effected by Eliot"
(*OBCV* xlxvi), are everywhere apparent in his work. To
some extent he is, while not exactly derivative, at least
prone to over-appreciation of others' mannerisms and
styles. On occasion it is difficult to be sure if a poem is
deliberate pastiche, or unconscious echo not only of man-
ner, but of this or that particular poem as in his "Ode: on
the death of William Butler Yeats." Sometimes, though,
intent is deliberate and the result is a poem; instance the
lovely "To Henry Vaughan." And it would be hard to
find more felicitous echo and appreciation, plus unob-
trusive erudition, than in "To Jay Macpherson on Her
Book of Poems":

> You flick the willow rod and cast the fly;
> And when the silver fish is caught and drawn,
> How neat the table he's divided on,
> How white the cloth, how elegant the dish,
> How sweet the flesh—O sacramental Fish!

Savoury—then one's eye flicks back, and how much more
savoury the ironical double entendre, the packed mytho-
logical reminiscences of the poem's first line, "Dear no-
man's-nightingale, our Fisher Queen." Here maiden
poetess and Odysseus' siren jostle for room in an image
which, on the face of it, could even be denial that Miss
Macpherson is a poet at all. The last two words in that
line not only introduce the fishy imagery permeating the
whole, but prepare for an "elegant" Grail and its sacra-
mental content in the last line of the poem (for it is one)
which summons up memory of the Eucharistic Fish in a
Last Supper in Ravenna's Church of San Appollonare
Nuovo (c. 510-520 A.D.).

Similarly successful is "Souvenirs du Temps Perdu"
where echoes bounce from Yeats to Eliot via Chesterton's
"Lepanto," from Browning to "yes sir she's my baby" of
the twenties—all put into one mouth, that of a washroom
drunk who leaves something in (what?) bowl as he (how?)
passes out. Here quotation and echo of other men's words

show not merely verbal facility but acquire underlying meaning, a disturbing inner life of their own.

It is evident that A. J. M. Smith is an academic poet, a learned poet, a poet's poet—all as others have said. But there are two sides to his coinage. He is also a poet, who can, when he chooses or when the grave white goddess decrees, touch through to leave nourishment such as Athena did in Achilles' furious heart. Smith's "Bridegroom," for example, who goes among "slaves of workmen strained," takes upon

> . . . his creased brow
> The sweat of these.
> The only peace
> That he shall know
> Is love of these. . . .

Not all Smith's poems are this "individual and penetrating" and one is left with a general impression of cosmopolitan anonymity since, in place of being first personal and local, reaching out then through man to men to compass a universe, Smith's work is cosmopolitan in intent and therefore, lacking deep roots, so much the less a living thing.

In his *Book of Canadian Poetry* (1943) he states "poetry must be written by the whole man"—which is so. Twelve years later during the Canadian Writers' Conference at Queen's University in 1955, he declared that "the audience a poet writes for . . . is primarily other poets." (*Writing in Canada*: Proceedings . . . ed. George Whalley, p. 20). Here he echoed Graves who, in a foreword to his *Poems 1938-45*, claimed to "write poems for poets. . . . For people in general I write prose. . . . To write poems for other than poets is wasteful." The statement was queried. Discussion followed, and after polling the group Earle Birney announced that "No poet in our group, except Miss Jay Macpherson, admitted to writing primarily for poets" (p. 47).

Yet Graves and Smith speak partial truth: the true poet

writes for himself alone—but for that self which, by extension, can include all men, dead, living, unborn.

Here Smith's equivocal status proves a poor prop. As a lapsed Catholic does not necessarily turn Mormon, Methodist, Muslim—what have you?—so he who puts by his national consciousness, or conscience, does not *ipso facto* become another-national. He can remain colloidally suspended, belonging nowhere, while yet unable to escape an involvement of sorts with, an investment by, immediate environment. To misquote, "For the poet living abroad, there are two things he cannot be detached from—his personality and his environment." Yet apparently Smith's only overt mention of Yankeedom is in "Eden's Isle" (1956), an otherwise flat and dated piece of verse where

> The Eagle rides on the storm;
> His shadow blots out the Isle.

On the other hand his much anthologized "The Lonely Land" is a crystallization of Canada few writers have equalled. Yet does it not rather read in reverse? Is it not the persona of the poem who is lonely for the land?

> A wild duck calls
> to her mate,
> and the ragged
> and passionate tones
> stagger and fall. . . .

Smith has another poem to the North which one must envy him. Here he is consciously the smith, the forger, the maker. Again he uses favourite image and adjective. "I will take words," he says,

> As crisp and white
> As our snow . . .
> As young as a trillium, and old
> As Laurentia's long undulant line . . .
> To hold . . .
> Lonely, unbuyable, dear,
> The North, as a deed, and forever.

Another poet—also, like Anderson, an incomer to Canada
—has said: "A poet must belong somewhere so intensely
that in his belonging that somewhere comes to belong to
him. But this involvement to the point of mutual pos-
session, interpenetration, must be not only with 'the
country of his own head'."— (P. K. Page, in *Preview*.) That
is the danger Smith has courted, involvement only with
"the country of his own head." Has he by long residence
on foreign soil become so imbued with *spiritum adop-
tionis filiorum* (Rom. 8) as to be a landless man?

"Pax mundi singed and signed and sealed" (76) : out of
context that numbed line, the sardonic universal peace,
perhaps best expresses the final state of that exile who,
unlike Athenian, Florentine, Dubliner, accepts whole-
heartedly the "adoption of sons" so that if not reasoning
head, at least the more surely instinctive heart is indeed
"cooled, cold, killed" (76) .

Or has this man turned residential circumstances to
good account, bringing ". . . the special, painful clarity of
exile to the common task of all modern artists . . . to define
their relation to their country, and their country's relation
to its own past" (*Time* LXXVII 22 [May 26/61]) ? Despite
"The Lonely Land" and a few other poems, it does not
appear so. Smith, lacking absorption into, identification
with, place, is not in full truth a Canadian poet.

That is not quite to name him apostate. He is indeed an
apostle of Canadian literature, and by his criticism and
anthologizing has done more for the making of that litera-
ture than many a better poet; and in completely gaining
the poet Canada might have lost the critic who so well
serves her. One can but hope that Smith will long survive
his *Collected Poems* to give to this country of his birth
more in both the criticism yet so sorely needed—and in
creation: "The North, as a deed, and forever." For some
of Smith's poems do have that air: in themselves, deeds;
deed also to the holding he has staked out in the realms of

Canadian literature. One remembers a poem of the calibre of "Astraea Redux":

> Coming over the water
> paddling an old boat
> with broken board . . .
> Coming to land
> coming home
> to the good people
> known anew
> My people   lordly ones
> the Duke of Dudek   His Grace of Layton
> and with me Scott
> diaconal,
> Known anew,   loved always
> . . . always . . . now . . .
> Memo: Note to go on my travels again

Perhaps Arthur Smith has been "singed and signed and sealed" by *patria*, and cannot escape even if he would; and though his travels in the body may continue, heart may return "to the good people/known anew."

REVIEW OF A. J. M. SMITH'S

COLLECTED POEMS

GEORGE WOODCOCK

In London during the 1930s there were two Canadian poets whose names had somehow penetrated the Atlantic fogs and had become familiar to English versifiers and verse-readers. One we knew because he was insistently among us. This was Paul Potts, who called himself "The

From "Turning New Leaves" by George Woodcock. From *Canadian Forum*, XLII (February 1963), 257-8. Copyright 1963 by *Canadian Forum*. Reprinted by permission of *Canadian Forum* and the author.

Canadian hick poet," and sold broadsheets of his verses
near the speakers' pitches in Hyde Park; later, in the
Forties, when Tambimuttu reigned as the leading poetic
impresario in England, Potts had his brief moment of
recognition, and then passed out of the light. In Canada,
as far as I can gather, he never even passed into the light.
A more enigmatic, but obviously a more substantial poet,
was A. J. M. Smith, whose work at that time was arousing
the interest of the late Thirties sophisticates and was being
published in the magazines edited by Geoffrey Grigson
(*New Verse*) and Julian Symons (*Twentieth Century
Verse*). Few people seemed even to know that he was a
Canadian, and it was another decade before Howard
Sergeant's efforts to bring Commonwealth poets to the
attention of English readers made the London literary
world at all aware of Smith's importance as an influence on
the more vital trends of writing in this country.

Smith's poetry, in fact, had made its way to acceptance
independently of his background. He became recognized
abroad as a poet worth watching almost before he was
widely known at home, and, with the possible and dubious
exception of Morley Callaghan, he was the first among
those we now regard as the important Canadian writers of
our time to receive such recognition. His *Collected Poems*,
which have just been published by the Oxford University
Press, completely sustain the tentative judgments of the
Thirties. Smith is not merely a poet who has sustained
astonishingly over three decades the quality of his writing;
he is also a poet whose retrospective harvest at the end of
that period awakens exactly the same fresh response as his
earlier poems did when one encountered them in his and
one's own youth. There are few poets whose work keeps
well over a generation; Smith is one of them, and in my
view the present volume places him clearly among the
more memorable lyric poets writing in our time, not
merely in Canada, but in the whole English-speaking
world.

This is all the more surprising since Smith has discarded very little in making his collection. The *Collected Poems* include almost the whole of the earlier volumes—*News of the Phoenix* and *A Sort of Ecstasy*—as well as a small group of poems written over the past decade. Smith has avoided a chronological arrangement, and his gathering of the poems according to manner and mood rather than time emphasises his remarkable sustenance of both emotional intensity and the lapidary craftsmanship he has always sought,

> . . . as hard
> And as smooth and as white
> As a brook pebble cold and unmarred. . . .

Smith, in fact, is a poet little bound by time or place. Even the poems he wrote during the Thirties, when the influence of the current movement was so pervasive, are remarkably undated; there is nothing of the comradely fustiness that nowadays stales so much of the early Spender or Day Lewis. Indeed, if there is anything that Smith retains to place him in the period through which he has worked and lived, it is a slight rococo tang that reminds one of the Twenties rather than of the later decades in which almost all his verse was written. Yeats and the Sitwells are much more his natural siblings than Auden and his circle. Perhaps Smith was saved from the vagaries of literary fashion by time and place of birth alike. He is older than any of the leading Thirties poets and was already shaping his literary *persona* when they appeared, while he was never subjected to the rather stultifying London coterie atmosphere which, in my view, prevented so many of the younger men whose work appeared beside his in the magazines of the latter part of the decade from developing their potentialities in any fullness. (Apart from Dylan Thomas, the only poets emerging at that time whom I would now put on a level with Smith on the grounds of sustained achievements are Roy Fuller and Kathleen Raine.)

If the world Smith creates in his poems is autonomous
in time—a kind of poetic Laputa that might dip down as
easily in the seventeenth century as in the twentieth to
which its navigator inalienably belongs—it seems equally
free in place. There are, admittedly, a very few poems in
the collected volumes which it must be hard for the non-
Canadian to apprehend.

> My people   lordly ones
> the Duke of Dudek His Grace of Layton
> and with me Scott
> diaconal, archbishopric
> twisted benevolent
> with needle eye

says a poem on the Keewaydin Poetry Conference, but
such parochial cosiness is rare. Smith, it is true, declares
his intention

> To hold in a verse as austere
> As the spirit of prairie and river,
> Lonely, unbuyable, dear,
> The North, as a deed, and for ever.

But even his rather imagistic poems on Canadian land-
scapes have none of the guidebook topography one some-
times encounters in writers like Birney and Gustafson.
The elements that Smith uses may have been abstracted
from the Canadian landscape; the result is a glimpse into
the same detached and personal world as that where (in
Smith's only apparently less literal poems) the Phoenix
does not die, "The Bellow of good Master Bull/As-
toundeth gentil Cow. . . ." and "Mrs. bloody Bikini Balls"
cuts off "poor Edward's nuts." The familiar cedar and firs
and wild ducks' calls in a poem like "The Lonely Land"
lead us into a landscape in its feeling as mythological as
any painted by Poussin for the encounters of Gods and
mortals.

> This is a beauty
> of dissonance
> this resonance
> of stony strand,

> this smoky cry
> curled over a black pine
> like a broken
> and wind-battered branch
> when the wind
> bends the tops of the pines
> and curdles the sky
> from the north.

Smith divides his book into five sections which, for lack of titles, I would describe as Yeatsian Philosophical, Imagistic, Rococo Pastoral, Satire and Parody, and Metaphysical Contemplation of Death. Such titles suggest derivativeness in Smith, which I hardly think he would deny. His debt to Yeats is clear, and leads him to include an Ode on the poet's death which, with its all too obvious swan that "leaps singing into the cold air," is one of the least fortunate of his poems. But the same bird and other birds—the dove and pigeon, crow and catbird, duck and swallow—sing much more winningly in his other verses, and the avian identification ("Only the raucous bird was something apart,/ As alien to all these/ As that other foul bird, my black heart") proclaims more truly his closeness to the poet of "the great wings beating still/ Above the staggering girl." In fact, the myth of Leda fascinates Smith as much as it did Yeats.

But originality, I can imagine Smith saying, if he has not actually done so, is an illusion of the half-baked pseudo-Romantic. Experience provides the raw material for all writings, and experience is never wholly original; the experience of a literary man, particularly, includes all the books he has read and all the poems that—good or bad —have sent the shivers down his spine. Hence, like Joyce and Eliot and Pound of the half-generation just before him, Smith resorts to those sublime forms of literary criticism—the only fully creative ones: the parody, the translation (there are excellent renderings of Gautier and Mallarmé), the deliberate pastiche (the "Souvenir de

Temps Perdu" written for Leon Edel), and the tribute in the manner of (finely rendered in "To Henry Vaughan"). All these are more than feats of imitative virtuosity; they are the emphatic approaches of a poet who can, when he desires, be resoundingly himself.

Smith's aims are spareness, clarity, balance, the austerity of a latter-day classicism enriched by the discoveries of the Symbolists and the Imagists. Unlike the wildly intuitive versifier he celebrates in "One Sort of Poet," Smith never sings, "Let it come! Let it come!" His poems are carefully worked to the last safe moment of polishing. One is aware of the unending search for words that are "crisp and sharp and small," for a form as "skintight" as the stallions of "Far West." Occasionally the visions clarified through Smith's bright glass are too sharp for comfort, the detachment too remote for feelings to survive. More often they are saved by the dense impact of the darker shapes that lie within the crystal, the

> shadows I have seen, of me deemed deeper,
> That backed on nothing in the horrid air.

It is this enduring sense of the shapeless beyond shape that gives Smith's best poems their peculiar rightness of tension, and make his austerities so rich in implication.

REVIEW OF A. J. M. SMITH'S
POEMS, NEW AND COLLECTED

LIONEL KEARNS

The next time I am trying to dissuade one of my students from honouring in English Literature I will give him something to read out of A. J. M. Smith's *New and Collected Poems*, for Smith's work seems to typify what can happen to an art form when it is dominated by an historically oriented academic discipline. After reading this volume I have no doubt that Smith knows exactly what he is doing, that his skill at playing the versification game matches his long established reputation, and that this kind of literary competence is of very little consequence to me or the world in which I live.

For the most part Smith relies on the time-worn gimmicks of traditional rhyme and regular metre, usually heavily iambic, to give his pieces poetic unity and mark them as verse. In keeping with this conventional approach he delights in figures of speech, abstract and lofty diction, classical allusions, inverted turns of phrase, generalized emotion, and occasionally gentlemanly wit. It is true that Smith has a certain flexibility of form; his models range from the Seventeenth Century Metaphysicals to Auden, Yeats and Eliot. The collection even contains a small section of imagistic nature poems in free verse, and these I found relatively pleasant. However, there is very little going on that is new or original. Everything is a kind of pastiche:

> Celestial strings might not surpass
> Thy morning breezes in long grass;
> The slow rain from the laden tree
> Dropping from heaven, brought to thee
> Sounds of purest harmony.

Here Smith reproduces the flavour of Henry Vaughan, whom he is celebrating. It is a clever exercise, but to what end? Even Smith's themes are run-of-the-mill literary when one finally chews through the reams of metaphor that dutifully obscure them: a low-keyed concern with love, death, and creation, spattered with smug erudition and polite unenthusiastic Christianity.

Perhaps the fact that I am not tuned in on A. J. M.'s

From "If There's Anything I Hate It's Poetry" by Lionel Kearns. From *Canadian Literature*, 36 (Spring 1968), 67-8. Copyright 1968 by *Canadian Literature*. Reprinted by permission of *Canadian Literature* and the author.

wave length colours my evaluation of these poems. I am ready to admit that others are sometimes capable of enjoying what I find inexorably dull, and I trust that persons with tastes differing from my own will find this collection more to their liking. The bad humour that it prompts in me personally stems, I believe, from the conviction that a major poet should be capable of doing a great deal more, of writing, for example, poems which are direct and "unpoetic" enough to be somehow symptomatic of human emotion. "Only the simplest words have meaning" choruses Smith in a poem on the death of E. J. Pratt, yet elsewhere in the collection he shows himself to be unconcerned with that kind of meaning. Perhaps truth is irrelevant in contexts where Smith believes poetry should operate. It depends, I suppose, on what a person thinks poetry is, and what he wants to do with it.

SECOND AND THIRD THOUGHTS
ABOUT SMITH

MILTON WILSON

According to T. S. Eliot, we learn to distrust the favourite poets of our adolescence. To this custom he attributes some of his uneasy feelings about Shelley. As an adolescent, I couldn't have cared less about Shelley, but my favourite Canadian poet was called Smith. I encountered him in that invaluable anthology *New Provinces*, which, at the beginning of the war, virtually *was* contemporary Canadian poetry to someone who, like me, had only recently discovered that it actually existed. But I don't attribute my second thoughts about Smith mainly to premature exposure: I just started to read his criticism.

"Second And Third Thoughts About Smith" by Milton Wilson. From *Canadian Literature*, 15 (Winter 1963), 11-17. Copyright 1963 by *Canadian Literature*. Reprinted by permission of *Canadian Literature* and the author.

I read it looking for the wrong things and distracted by the Smith legend already growing up around his "difficult, lonely music." Much of his terminology struck me as deriving from an Eliot either misunderstood or vulgarized, and I attributed an exaggerated importance to Smith's minor habits of speech. Take "classical," for example, which is really more of a Smith legend than a favourite Smith term, and which he generally replaces with such supposed equivalents as "austere," "disciplined," "concise," etc. T. S. Eliot let us know in an unguarded moment that his critical ideals were classical, but he never claimed that the term had much application to his own poems, or to those of his leading contemporaries. Indeed, he took pains to deny it. But Smith seemed to find the classical role congenial and even possible, although he can hardly be blamed for the extremes to which Pacey has taken him in it, any more than for Collin's earlier attempt to turn him into a "spiritual athlete" or desperate mystic. Certainly you don't have to talk to Smith for long to realize that he relishes the thought of being odd classical man out in a society of romantics, and, from the jacket blurb of his *Collected Poems*, we once again learn, presumably with the author's sanction, that he knows how to be "austerely classical" in his own graceful way. It's something of a let-down to discover how merely Parnassian or decadent or imagistic his classicism can be. Smith's less diffuse Medusa (in "For Healing") isn't that different from Swinburne's, his Hellenic swallows from H.D.'s, or even his Pan from Carman's. It is tempting (as I discovered in reviewing Smith's second collection of poems eight years ago) to resign this particular legend to the limbo of Auden's Oxford:

> And through the quads dogmatic words rang clear:
> "Good poetry is classic and austere."

More obtrusive and far less legendary in the Smith terminology is "metaphysical" and all the phrases that Eliot (himself the heir to a long line of nineteenth-century

critical formulas, as Frank Kermode points out) has taught
us to trail along behind it: the "disparate experience,"
"passion and thought" or "sense and intellect," "fused"
into a "unified sensibility." It hardly seems to matter
whether Smith is writing a jacket blurb on John Glassco,
analyzing Ronald Hambeton's "Sockeye Salmon," impro-
vising on Margaret Avison, addressing a conference of
librarians on contemporary Canadian literature in general,
reviewing *Towards the Last Spike,* or introducing Alfred
Bailey's work by telling us how well his "learning" is
"fused" with his "sensibility and feeling": the same
formula automatically recurs. Indeed, it is so persistently
and widely applied that in the end one balks at trying to
understand what he means by Anne Wilkinson's "meta-
physical romanticism" as much as by Wilfred Watson's
"classical precision of form."

But how relevant are my second thoughts? Do unskilful
classification and a perfunctory terminology really stand
in the way of Smith's critical achievement? Not, I think,
if we recognize where his real and remarkable virtues as
a critic lie and refuse to demand what he has no intention
of giving in the first place. Smith's key terms and classifica-
tions are useful only because, having provided something
of the sort, he can then feel free to exercise his best talents
elsewhere. The distinction between the natives and the
cosmopolitans, on which Smith hung the organization of
much of the first edition of *A Book of Canadian Poetry,*
has in the latest edition been silently dropped, with no
loss to the virtues of a difficult task finely carried out. He
is lucky to have discovered, and been encouraged to take
on, the rôle for which his critical skills best suit him. He
seems born to be an anthologizer, not of familiar, well-
stocked and well-combed fields, but of virgin territory;
he is happily doomed to exercise his finely perceptive and
carefully developed faculty of choice on the dubious, the
unpromising, the untried and the provincial, and by his
example to show his readers that such a choice is both

possible and necessary. Before Smith, Canadian anthologies were either uncritical appendages to national aspiration or simply of "the vacuum cleaner type" (as a reviewer has remarked of a recent example). Here are Smith's own words in 1939, when he was just starting to work on *A Book of Canadian Poetry*. "Discrimination has never been an essential part of a Canadian anthologist's equipment. Enthusiasm, industry, sympathy, yes; but taste, no." In the successive editions of the *Book* and in the more recent *Oxford Book of Canadian Verse*, he has given us a model of discrimination and scrupulous choice, which is salutary even for those whose preferences are very different from his. Smith offers no hard-won aesthetic principles, no freshly cleaned critical concepts, no brilliant arguments to inevitable conclusions; but one cannot read his Canadian anthologies (introduction and critical apparatus included) without responding to the firm, delicately sharpened, continuous pressures of a mind exercising its powers on materials which he finds half-alien and grudging in their Victorian beginnings, and perhaps equally alien, if a good deal richer, in their post-war ends, but which he manages somehow to coerce into satisfying the personal demands that he started with. I respond to the same process in his best essays and reviews, like the recent one on D. C. Scott in *Canadian Literature* and on Margaret Avison in the *Tamarack Review*. In reading the Scott essay, once I have repressed a few gestures of annoyance at the old surface habits (there is far too much invocation of that most delusive of standards, the "accurate image"), I can experience with great pleasure and profit his untwisting and discriminating and reweaving of the threads of Scott's sensibility, his finely selected anthology of quotations, and his convincing sympathy with a poetic mind whose qualities, I realize with something of a shock, are very like his own. He is equally discriminating on the diction and imagery of Margaret Avison, with whose centrifugal poetics and subordination of poem written to poem writing (she has almost no sense of authorial "natural piety"), he can have very little in common at all, although, of course, he manages to feel steady by invoking the "fusion" of "sensation and thought" in her "undissociated sensibility."

Smith, then, is a critic who stands or falls by purity of perception alone. He has a critical sense so fine (to adapt Eliot's famous remark on James) that it is incapable of being violated by an idea or even the lack of one. Far from being an intellectual critic, or (as he would no doubt prefer) a "unified" or "whole" one, he shows what can be done, and perhaps can only be done, by sharpening taste at the expense of its critical companions. But he shows this not only in writing criticism. As I read the *Collected Poems* which Oxford has just given us, I realize, as I never did before, just how all-of-a-piece, as well as how varied, Smith's work really is. "Metaphysical poetry and pure poetry are what I stand for," he has insisted. One may be justly dubious about his "metaphysical" qualities, but he is as pure a poet as he is a critic.

The hundred poems in this new collection come from forty years of work. It contains every poem but one from *News of the Phoenix* (38) and *A Sort of Ecstasy* (22) . The others (40) do include a few early, uncollected pieces, of which the longest and most interesting is "Three Phases of Punch," ninety per cent unchanged since its last appearance (as "Varia") in the *London Aphrodite* of April, 1929; but most of them, to the best of my knowledge, are the latest Smith. It is surely no longer necessary to waste time refuting the silliest of all the Smith legends: that his taste has stultified his invention and narrowed his range, that he has spent thirty years husbanding a minimum of creativity for a minimum of purposes. So I won't try to make a comprehensive survey of his long-sustained, inventive and remarkably varied output, which is certainly equal in range to that of any Canadian poet of his generation. Instead, I would prefer simply to watch the Smith "purity" at work in a few characteristic places, concentrating on what he does to other poets (the tributes, parodies, pastiches and translations), where the continuity of his poetry and criticism is likely to be most apparent, and pursuing the argument into adjacent areas wherever it seems useful.

The tributes are inseparable from the parodies, the parodies from the pastiches, and the pastiches from the translations. There must be at least twenty poems which belong somewhere within this continuity of categories, beginning with the ode to Yeats and the praise of Jay MacPherson at one end, followed by the revisioning of Vaughan and the *reducto ad absurdum* of George Johnston, moving through the glazed, wooden hyacinth for Edith Sitwell, the variations on Anne Wilkinson and the love song in Tom Moore tempo, continuing with the souvenir of the twenties, the Jacobean prothalamium and the lyric to a Catullan Anthea, and reaching at last the Gautier and Mallarmé translations at the other end. I cannot possibly think that Smith's translations are not as good English poems as the originals are French ones. In fact, what *could* be better than his version of "Brigadier"? And the high spirits of some of these pastiches are enough to convince even the most hidebound primitive that literature which claims to forswear precedent has no monopoly on vitality. What is more to my point, the process of discrimination and selection responsible for the anthologies and for the Scott and Avison essays can here be seen most clearly at work—in the lively redistorting mirror he provides for George Johnston, Tom Moore or Edith Sitwell, and in the more sober ecstasy that he filters through Anne Wilkinson or Henry Vaughan.

The Smith purity shows at its best in the admirable Vaughan poem, which is worth saving for the last. It works less convincingly on Yeats, as the somewhat faded intensities of the "Ode on the Death of W. B. Yeats" demonstrate. The obvious comparison is with Auden's "In Memory of

W. B. Yeats." Smith shares some Auden mannerisms, particularly in the handling of epithets (see the third stanza), but the nature of his poem is very different. Auden's rich, diffuse, sectional elegy tries to include a great deal—intellectual, political, psychological, aesthetic—not only of Yeats but of the world in which Yeats died, and of course he ruminates and draws a moral or two. Smith's Yeats, however, is purified of almost everything except a few basic images. But, instead of distilling the essence of a great poet (as the Vaughan tribute does), the "Ode" succeeds only in reducing a great poet to the level of his own clichés.

> A wild swan spreads his fanatic wing.
> Ancestralled energy of blood and power
> Beats in his sinewy breast. . . .
> The swan leaps singing into the cold air . . .
> . . . crying
> To the tumultuous throng
> Of the sky his cold and passionate song.

Even if it were one of Yeat's most convincing poses that Smith has taken over, one could still detect something of the stock response at work here. In another Smith poem, "On Reading an Anthology of Popular Poetry," we are told how

> The old eternal frog
> In the throat that comes
> With the words *mother, sweetheart, dog*
> Excites and then numbs.

In reading early Smith, I feel the same way about the word *cold*.

Fortunately, the *Collected Poems* allows the reader to put Smith's more ascetic mannerisms in perspective. The poet may protest too much, he may risk succumbing to a formula, he may even seem to imagine that he can escape from a soft cliché by exchanging it for a hard one, but his talent is too rich to allow doctrinaire confinement. The angularities of "The Lonely Land" do have their important share in Smith's "sort of ecstasy," but his sensibility achieves its fullest release when the crisp, clear, cold, smooth, hard, pointed, austere, lonely, etc. (I choose my list of adjectives from "To Hold a Poem") is complemented by the shimmer and fluctuation, the flash and fade, which Smith has helped us to perceive in D. C. Scott. "The Fountain," "Nightfall" and (especially) "The Circle" are more fully characteristic of Smith than "Swift Current" or "In the Wilderness" or even "The Lonely Land" itself.

If the Smith brand of purity works better in the Vaughan poem than it did in the Yeats, it is perhaps because in the former so much potential impurity is held in willing suspension.

> Homesick?   and yet your country Walks
> Were heaven'd for you.   Such bright stalks
> Of grasses!   such pure Green!

The gently puzzled and at first only half-comprehending tone in which Smith presents Vaughan's combination of homesickness for eternity with sensitiveness to the divinity of his place of exile (his peculiarly ungnostic gnosticism) is fully absorbed into a concentration and refinement of Vaughan's sensibility and idiom (Smith's extract of Vaughan—and a wonderful distillation it turns out to be), while the religious paradox

> (Yet thou art Homesick!   to be gone
> From all this brave Distraction
> Wouldst seal thine ear, nail down thine eyes . . .
> Thou art content to beg a pall,
> Glad to be Nothing, to be all.)

seems in the end so transparent as almost to be purified of religious meaning. But what the Smith purification of Vaughan makes only half-apparent (Vaughan, after all, is a pretty special case) is unmistakable if one sets Smith beside "that preacher from a cloud in Paul's," his favourite Donne, from whom our basic concept of a metaphysical

poet must necessarily come. Smith obviously lacks the
sheer argumentativeness, the sequential pressure of intel-
lectual give and take, the involvement in conceptual
definition and differentiation which gives Donne so much
of his flavour. What he possesses are such things as the
intellectual high spirits of the superb "What Casey Jones
Said to the Medium" or the forceful syntactic logic of
poems like "The Archer," "To a Young Poet," "The Flesh
Repudiates the Bone" and a good many others. I choose
one short enough to quote.

> This flesh repudiates the bone
>   With such dissolving force,
> In such a tumult to be gone,
>   Such longing for divorce,
> As leaves the livid mind no choice
>   But to conclude at last
> That all this energy and poise
>   Were but designed to cast
> A richer flower from the earth
>   Surrounding its decay,
> And like a child whose fretful mirth
>   Can find no constant play,
> Bring one more transient form to birth
>   And fling the old away.

If one must use the terminology of the sacred wood,
then what Smith gives us is less like Eliot's required
fusion of thought and emotion than like his "emotional
equivalent of thought." And if one can't resist a seven-
teenth-century title, there's always "cavalier" ready for
the taking. But the temptation had better be resisted.
Having watched Smith refuse to be contained by his own
formulas, I can hardly expect him to be contained by
mine. "The plot against Proteus" can be left to other
hands: "when you have him, call." In the meantime, the
continuous liveliness of texture in these *Collected Poems*
keeps rousing my prejudices—for and against. My third
thoughts about Smith are unlikely to be my last.

A SELF-REVIEW

A. J. M. SMITH

As a poet I am not the sort unenviously described in the lines beginning

> Though he lift his voice in a great O
> And his arms in a great Y.

When I write a poem I try to know what I am doing—at least with respect to craft. Luck is needed too, of course, and luck is unpredictable. All I know about it is that it has to be earned. Everything beneath the surface of technique remains obscure. It is this subterranean world, now that this book is out of my hands, I shall try to explore in these very tentative notes.

I remember a paradox of the psychology pundits: "How can I know what I think till I see what I say?" To apply this to the poet we need more verbs: *feel, fear, hope, love, hate*—an infinite series whose sum is *am* or *be*; so the question becomes for me "How do I know who I am till I hear what I write?"

> How all men wrongly death to dignify
> Conspire, I tell

Sounds differently from "I tell how all men conspire to dignify death wrongly," and expresses (or is) a different person. One can understand, then, that it is with a good deal of trepidation that I look into the handsome volume, as into a magnifying mirror, that is a credit at least to Mr. William Toye, the typographer and designer, and Mr. Theo Dimson, who drew the beautiful black and red Phoenix.

"A Self-Review" by A. J. M. Smith. From *Canadian Literature*, 15 (Winter 1963), 20-26. Copyright 1963 by *Canadian Literature*. Reprinted by permission of *Canadian Literature* and the author.

Some people may think it presumptuous to call a book of only a hundred short, mainly lyrical pieces of verse *Collected Poems*—but actually that is exactly what it is. Though I have a file full of verses in every stage of gestation from mere spawn to almost finished (that is, nearly *right*) poems, those in the book are all that I want to let out of my hands now, as being beyond my power to improve. Of these hundred, a few were written when I was an undergraduate and published in journals as different as *The McGill Fortnightly Review* and *The Dial*. And a few were written just the other day. Which is which would be hard to tell. Many of the poems, though started long ago and some of them printed in an unsatisfactory version, were not corrected or really finished (that is, not written) until years later—in one or two cases until I was correcting page proofs last summer. The second to last line of "Far West," for example, as it stands now was a happy afterthought,[1] which not only intensified the accuracy of the experience but got rid of a miserable echo of Cummings that had troubled my conscience ever since the poem was first published in England in the late thirties. The second couplet of the last stanza of "The Fountain" had never seemed quite inevitable, but many hours working over it in proof finally got it right—or at least I think so. Anyway, for better or worse, it remains, and now the third time round, the poem is written at last.

A really new poem, though made out of some very old sketches, is "The Two Birds." Working on the page proofs I became dissatisfied with a piece of technically accomplished and rather emotionally enervating word-music that second thoughts told me ought to be dropped. ("The Circle" and "Nightfall" were about all the traffic would bear of that sort.) Almost by chance I came on a batch of old *McGill Fortnightly Reviews* stacked away in the attic.

---

[1]The last two lines of *Far West* now run thus:

As the cowboys ride their skintight stallions
Over the barbarous hills of California.

Looking through them I found a long forgotten poem called "Something Apart." It was awkward, clumsy and undigested. There were some good lines in it but also some very trite phrases and hazy images. There was also one brief bit that had been taken over and worked into "The Lonely Land." But the poem consisted of three stanzas of seven lines each; and that was exactly the dimensions of the piece I wanted a subsitute for. So I started to work on the rediscovered sketches. I put a new ribbon in my typewriter, got a batch of typewriting paper and a couple of soft pencils, and started in. Suddenly, my imagination caught fire, and all the vague clichés of the thing began to drop away. I was able to organize it, tighten it, work out a development and bring it to a satisfying and unexpected close. The last lines had been particularly weak and sentimental. They told how the raucous bird was "something apart"—you have guessed it!—"from the sorrow in my heart." But now everything was changed—the title, which awakens a curiosity which is not satisfied until the last line (though a clue is dropped in the middle line of the middle stanza, "a voice as twisted as mine"); the image of the heart as a second foul bird; the "gold sun's winding stair" of the second stanza; and, last of all to be written, the title and the first word of the poem. *So,* to suggest an antecedent unspecified source of the bitterness, remorse, and self-disgust that the complete poem finally expresses. Unspecified, of course, because irrelevant—"another story," hinted at perhaps in the "Who is that bitter king? It is not I" of the first poem in the book and the reference to "this savory fatness" in "On Knowing 'Nothing'," one of the last. And here perhaps, with luck, will be the source of poems yet to be written.

You will see from all this that I do not believe in progress in the ordinary sense of the word. The more recent poems in this collection are neither "better" nor "worse" than the earlier, and what differences there are depend on the genre or the occasion, not on the time of writing. Such development as has occurred took place before the poem was printed. If the development was not marked enough then the piece remains in the notebook or file. The different voices and different modes called for by the different occasions should not obscure the underlying unity pervading even the most apparently different poems. "Ballade un peu Banale" is in one tone, "Good Friday" and "Canticle of St. John" are in another; but each is equally serious, and each modifies the others. The same is true of (say) "The Offices of the First and the Second Hour" and "Song Made in Lieu of Many Ornaments," the first a programme of asceticism and the second a playful but not frivolous treatment of the Pauline doctrine of holy matrimony. I agree with Geoffrey Grigson that there is no essential difference between an epic and a limerick. "You cannot suppose a divine or an inspired origin for one against a secular or rational origin for the other." Each must be equally well written; each must be as good as its author can make it. That is the function of the poet with respect to his poems. He is a craftsman, and for a great part of the time he is a conscious craftsman. It is only in the essential climatic moment (or hour) that the Muse takes over and the work goes on one cannot say how or why.

My poems are not, I think, autobiographical, subjective, or personal in the obvious and perhaps superficial sense. None of them is revery, confession or direct self-expression. They are fiction, drama, art; sometimes pastiche, sometimes burlesque, and sometimes respectful parody; pictures of possible attitudes explored in turn; butterflies, moths or beetles pinned wriggling—some of them, I hope— on the page or screen for your, and my, inspection. The "I" of the poem, the protagonist of its tragedy or the clown of its pantomime, is not me. As Rimbaud said, *Je est un autre,* I is another.

"Indeed?" I can hear you explain. "Then who *is* this collector of butterflies and bugs you have been describing?

Your emblem ought to be the chameleon or mole, not the Phoenix or swan."

You have a point all right. And it's an important one. It goes to the heart of the general problem of the role of personality, conscious and unconscious, in artistic creation —the problem, indeed, of personal responsibility. As a poet (no philosopher or moralist) I can only touch upon it lightly and indirectly—as in the poem "Poor Innocent":

> It is a gentle natural (is it I?) who
> Visits timidly the big world of
> The heart, &c.

The question is answered (or not answered) in the denouement of the little metaphysical comedy that is so well suited to the dynamics of the Italian sonnet:

> Back to your kennel, varlet! Fool, you rave!
> Unbind that seaweed, throw away that shell!

The controlling mind, the critical shaping faculty of the rational consciousness sends the tremulous instinctive and sensuous fancy packing.

It is this rather bossy intelligence which chooses what is to be expressed, considers how, and judges the final outcome. But what a lot escapes it—or cajoles it, or fools it! It did not choose the images, the metaphors, the sensations, or the sounds that chime and clash in the consonants and vowels—though it did eventually approve them. What or who was it, indeed, that suffered a sea-change so it could breathe in a world

> Where salt translucency's green branches bear
> This sea-rose, a lost mermaid, whose cold cave,
> Left lightness now, the lapping seatides lave
> At base of Okeanos' twisted stair

or watched

> What time the seamew sets
> Her course by stars among the smoky tides
> Entangled?

I do not know. Where *do* the images of a writer come from? From experience, I suppose. But not—in my case at least—from experience as emotion, and not remembered (that is, not *consciously* remembered) in tranquillity or otherwise. When, for instance, did I look up at an "icicle sharp kaleidoscopic white sky" or see "birds like dark star-light twinkle in the sky"? When did I gaze on "the gold sun's winding stair" in the deep pinewoods or see "the green hills caked with ice" under a bloodshot moon? I don't know when, but I must have, waking or in dream, and the experience sank into the depths of the Self to be dredged up heavens know how long afterwards.

I do remember—not any one specific moment, but as in a dream many times, always at evening or in the early morning, the swallows skimming over the rapids by the old mill at Laval-sur-le-Lac near Saint Eustache where we used to go for the summer when I was a child. I remember August 4th, 1914, there, and I remember helping to search for the body of a young man drowned in the rapids. And so the swallows, associated with loneliness and death by water, swerve into one or two of the more intimate of the poems and become a source of simile and metaphor. But why *crisp* should seem to be an obsessive word and *love* more than once evoke stinging whips I do not know.

Let us return to the known word of the consciousness. Irony and wit are intentional, and I note that there is one device of irony that I have seemed to find particularly congenial. This is ironic understatement or anti-climax, the intentional and rather insulting drop into bathos. This can be dangerous when turned upon oneself; ironic self-depreciation can be too easily taken by others as sober literal truth. But when turned against the knaves and fools who are the traditional targets of classical satire it can be very effective. I find a number of instances of it, however, whose intention or effect is less certain. I will try to take one or two of them apart to see how they work.

This may perhaps help the reader to know why he thinks them good or bad.

In the following lines from "Bird and Flower" the destructive criticism is concentrated in the bathos of the last word:

Some holy men so love their cells they make
.Their four gray walls the whole damned stinking world
And God comes in and fills it *easily*.

The paradox here is in the statement that God should find anything easy or (by implication therefore) hard. What we have actually is an inverted hyperbole calculated to emphasize how small and mean is the monastic world of the "holy" men who blaspheme the world of natural love. Only for them, not for the poet and the particular woman he is writing about, is the world a damned and stinking world.

There is a similar paradoxical misapplication of a limiting adverbial idea to the infinity of God in the comic poem "Ballade un peu Banale" where in order to take the virgin cow to heaven Christ is described as having to make use of "some miraculous device." This sort of thing is found, without irony, in many primitive Christian paintings. I find another application (this time without any pejoratve intention) of a similarly incongruous or limiting epithet on the lines "To Henry Vaughan"

Lifting the rapt soul out of Time
Into a *long* Eternity.

As applied to the infinite duration of Eternity *long* is understatement and bathos. Its purpose, however, is not to be ironic at the expense of the naivete of Henry Vaughan. Far from it. The poem is a genuine tribute to a wholly admirable poet and seer. The purpose of the figure is to convey as sharply as possible the identification of time and eternity (see also "The Two Sides of a Drum") in the mind of Vaughan as a mystic.

Where Heaven is now, and still to be.

I think this gets across for the reader who is sympathetic to Vaughan or to Christian or Platonic ideas. For one who is not (and the present writer is sometimes one such reader and sometimes the other) the effect of irony does come through after all, and gently indicates the noble futility of Vaughan's magnificent piety.

A couple of other instances of this device will emphasize how characteristic it seems to be. From "Noctambule"

> Reality at two removes, and mouse and moon
> *Successful.*

Merely successful, not triumphant or victorious or right or good, so that even mouse and moon (as well as lion and sun) suffer from the deprivation that it is the main business of the poem to lament.

And in "The Common Man":

> At first he thought this helped him when he tried
> To tell who told the truth, who plainly lied.

The hyperbole in the idea that it is a matter of great difficulty to tell who *plainly* lied is the concisest way of suggesting the confusion of values in the modern world of political propaganda, mass media brainwashing, and cold-war bilge. Though this poem was written in the mid forties it has got truer every decade and is another version of the ironic series of events outlined in the angry political poems on the threat of nuclear suicide.

It is obvious that there is much here that is consciously contrived; much too whose author, a greater poet might say, is in eternity. How good either is, it is not for me to say. I hope every reader of this piece will buy the book and judge for himself.

SELECTED BIBLIOGRAPHY

Surveys of Canadian literature which place the poets dealt with in this collection in historical perspective include *The Literary History of Canada,* ed. Carl F. Klinck (Toronto: University of Toronto Press, 1965) and Desmond Pacey's *Creative Writing in Canada* (Toronto: The Ryerson Press, rev. ed. 1961). Books devoted more specifically to these poets are

Collin, W. E. *The White Savannahs,* Toronto: Macmillan, 1936. This book contains a separate chapter on each of the poets:

      Scott: "Pilgrim of the Absolute," 177-204.
      Smith: "Difficult Lonely Music," 235-263.
      Kennedy: "This Man of April," 267-284.

Pacey, Desmond. *Ten Canadian Poets.* Toronto: The Ryerson Press, 1958.

This book contains chapters on A. J. M. Smith (194-222) and F. R. Scott (223-253).

The list of articles below contains articles of critical comment by the poets themselves, together with replies to those comments. The list also includes review articles on their poetry.

Birney, Earl. "A.J.M.S.," *Canadian Literature,* 15 (Winter 1963), 4-6.

Brinnin, John Malcolm. "Views of Favorite Mythologies," *Poetry,* LXV (December 1944), 157-160.

Brown, E. K. "Canadian Poetry Repudiated: Review of *New Provinces,*" *New Frontier,* I (July 1936), 31-32.

———. "Review of *News of the Phoenix,*" *University of Toronto Quarterly,* XIII (April 1944), 308-309.

Dudek, Louis. "Review of Smith's *Collected Poems,*" *Delta,* 20 (February 1963), 27-28.

Duncan, Chester. "Review of *Eye of the Needle,*" *Tamarack Review,* 3 (Spring 1957), 81-82.

Fuller, Roy. "A Poet of the Century," *Canadian Literature,* 15 (Winter 1963), 7-10.

Gnarowski, Michael. "The Role of the Little Magazine in the Development of Poetry in English in Montreal," *Culture,* XXIV (September 1963), 274-286.

Kennedy, Leo. "The Future of Canadian Literature," *Canadian Mercury,* I (April-May, 1929), 99-100.

Klein, A. M. "The Poetry of A. J. M. Smith," *Canadian Forum,* XXIII (February 1944), 257-258.

Livesay, Dorothy. "Review of *News of the Phoenix,*" *First Statement,* II (April 1944), 18-19.

Scott, F. R. "A. J. M. Smith," *Leading Canadian Poets,* ed. W. P. Percival (Toronto: The Ryerson Press, 1948), 234-244.

———. "A Note on Canadian War Poetry," *Preview,* 9 (November, 1942), 3-5.

———. Letter in reply to "Wanted — Canadian Criticism," *Canadian Forum*, VIII (June 1928), 697-698.

"F. R. Scott's *Overture*" (an unsigned review), *Canadian Poetry Magazine*, IX (September 1945), 33-35.

Shaw, Neufville. "The Maple Leaf Is Dying — A Review of Smith's *Book of Canadian Poetry*," *Preview*, 17 (December 1943), 1-3.

Smith, A. J. M. "A Note on Metaphysical Poetry," *Canadian Mercury*, I (February 1929), 61-62.

———. "A Rejected Preface," *Canadian Literature*, 24 (Spring 1965), 6-9.

———. "Contemporary Poetry," *McGill Fortnightly Review*, II (December 15, 1926), 31-32.

———. "Electic Detachment," *Canadian Literature*, 9 (Summer 1961), 6-14.

———. "Preface," *A Book of Canadian Poetry*, (Toronto: Gage, 1943), 3-34.

———. "Symbolism in Poetry," *McGill Fortnightly Review*, I (December 5, 1925), 11-12 and 16.

———. "The Poet," *Writing In Canada*, ed. George Whalley (Toronto: Macmillan, 1956), 13-24.

———. "Wanted — Canadian Criticism," *Canadian Forum*, VIII (April 1928), 600-601.

Sutherland, John. "The Old And The New," Introduction to *Other Canadians* (Montreal: First Statement Press, 1947), 5-20.

———. "Review of Smith's *Book of Canadian Poetry*", *First Statement*, II (April 1944), 19-20.

———. "The Two Schools," *First Statement*, II (August 1943), 1-3.

Wilson, Milton. "Review of Smith's *Collected Poems*," *University of Toronto Quarterly*, XXXII (July 1963), 371-373.